The N 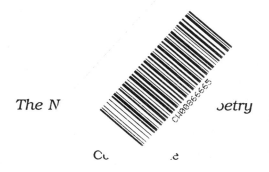 *ɔetry*

Cɔ   .e

The Norton Anthology of Poetry
Third Edition

Course Guide
for the Complete and Shorter Editions

Debra Fried
Cornell University

W • W • NORTON & COMPANY • INC •

New York   London

ISBN 0-393-95247-9

W. W. Norton & Company, Inc., 500 Fifth Avenue, New York, N.Y. 10110
W. W. Norton & Company Ltd., 37 Great Russell Street, London WC1B 3NU

2 3 4 5 6 7 8 9 0

CONTENTS

INTRODUCTION: THE ANTHOLOGY AS TEXTBOOK

This Course Guide is designed to suggest ways of using *The Norton Anthology of Poetry*, Third Edition, as a textbook in introductory courses in poetry. An anthology cannot possess the neat pedagogic order of a syllabus, in part because an anthology has at least two sets of authors: the poets who, over many centuries, wrote the selections, and the editors who chose and arranged them. In *The Last Gentleman*, Walker Percy nicely observes his double parentage: "From the anthology there arose a subtler smell, both exotic and businesslike, of the poet's disorder, his sweats and scribblings, and of the office order of the professor and his sweet ultimate ink." I hope that this Course Guide will be both exotic and businesslike enough to be of value to a third set of authors, the instructors who will select and rearrange the poems— anthologize them, we might as well say— for their own classroom uses. It is intended not as a handbook of classroom procedures, but as a reference book for teachers that will enable them to find their way around in the anthology, as well as to propose a diversity of possible ways to select, group, and discuss the poems that it includes.

Using This Guide

The Norton Anthology of Poetry arranges poems chronologically by authors, an ordering designed to make it easy to locate an individual poet, and also to give students a rough idea of historical sequence and the evolution of poetic forms, devices, and subjects. But I imagine most of us who teach poetry to undergraduates will wish to impress on our students that a literary tradition can be understood in other ways than by proceeding from the anonymous "Cuckoo Song" straight through to the lyrics of Leslie Marmon Silko. Students will certainly be more astute readers of "The Cuckoo Song" if they read it in the context of the other medieval lyrics included in this anthology, but they are likely to enjoy it more, and to see more point in studying it, if they also discover that "The Cuckoo Song" is not an isolated chirp, but part of a chorus of poetic birdsongs, written in all poetic eras. We can, for example, better teach our students to distinguish the particular tone of the cuckoo's "murie" call in the anonymous early lyric if we enable them to listen at the same time to the cuckoo's "word of fear" in Shakespeare's spring song from *Love's Labour's Lost*. And it should help students to see why both these poems repeat the cuckoo's cry in the same part of the poem if they read them in the context of other poems using refrain, a group that in turn includes a number of other songs celebrating the arrival of spring. My main procedure throughout the Guide has been to group birds of a feather, with the understanding that there are many kinds of plumage that poems display and according to which they may be classified in alternative ways. Thus "The Cuckoo Song" is listed three times here: in Section 4, Patterns, Structures, and Schemes, under Refrains; in Section 5, Language, Voice, and Address, under Address and Apostrophe; and in Section 7, Topics in the Poems, under Seasons and Seasonal Change (Spring). Many poems will reappear in this way under a number of headings, usually grouped once with poems that have similar structures or that exemplify similar features of versification, then grouped again with poems that concern similar subjects or that raise related issues in the teaching of poetry, such as diction or tone. Other poems will appear in only one category, and some poems in the anthology are not listed in this Guide at all. All the listings and examples are intended to be merely suggestive; alternative schemes and examples are left to the preference of the individual instructor.

There is thus nothing peremptory, final, or exhaustive about these groupings of poems, or about the arrangement of the lists. And each group can occupy any desired amount of time in a course: from a passing reference to a class session, a week, or even several weeks. While I tried to arrange this Guide according to a rough sequential logic of classroom presentation, I have also tried to suggest the variety of other ways in which a poetry course might be organized. The first three sections of this Guide list poems according to the features of Versification (Section 1) and the traditional Stanzas (Section 2) and Forms and Genres (Section 3) that they exemplify; the instructor may well want to spend time early in the course on such basic matters concerning the ways that poems are formed and put together. But it can make equally good sense to begin with some of the formal issues raised in Section 4, Patterns, Structures, and Schemes, or with the linguistic ones in Section 5, Language, Voice, and Address, and in Section 6, Figurative Language. Alternatively, before you ask students to think about how a poem is structured or the ways it uses language, you may want them to think about the subjects or occasions on which poems get written at all, and thus turn first to Section 7, Topics in the Poems. Examining the range of responses poets have expressed to something that students have experienced for themselves (the seasons, city life, love, solitude) is one good way to introduce questions of structure and language. For instance, what different views of love do we find in different genres? How do poems about love draw upon the poet's inventiveness in language, in comparisons and figurations? What different modes of address, even what sorts of metrical innovations and conventions, are illustrated by poems about love? Alternatively, asking students to read and compare poems about animals can be a way of introducing them to the significance of patterns and rhetorical schemes: Why does Blake confront the tiger by asking a battery of questions, while

Shelley addresses the skylark by testing a series of likenesses? A course that began with a selection of poems written by Minority Voices (Section 9), such as Black Poets (9.2) or Women Poets (9.1), could start by raising issues of the central or marginal status of poetry in the dominant culture, and perhaps move to the relations between the powers of poetic voice and the dominant culture's Traditions, Innovations, and Revisions (Section 8). Because each section of the Guide implies issues that are raised more explicitly in others, instructors should find it simple to select and arrange lists from each section in the order that will best suit the design of their courses. In most cases, the lists contain more poems than any instructor will wish to teach in a single course; it is expected that instructors will focus on only some of the poems from a list in class discussions, although they may want also to bring students' attention to others as supplementary reading, or for essay assignments, in-class reports, and other exercises.

The most challenging task in preparing a course may be the job of reshuffling these lists into a coherent syllabus; uncharitably enough, this task is left to the instructor. I hope that the lists will suggest other possible groupings and prompt the invention of new ways to introduce poetry to beginning students. But of course these lists are not innocent: the mere act of categorizing a poem imposes an interpretation on it, and urges a method of teaching it as well. One principle this Guide implicitly favors is that it is more effective to compare poems than to teach them in isolation: two poems make a better lesson than one. The reasons for this bias are obvious, perhaps, but worth rehearsing anyway. On the simplest pedagogic level, beginning students who may be somewhat hesitant to contrtibute to a discussion about one poem will often find it easier to respond when they are asked in a specific way to compare two poems. More importantly, teaching poems in conjunction is one way of encouraging students to reflect on how poems may engage the history of poetry, to understand that poets do not write as though no poems had ever been written before, but that poems may be simultaneously occasioned by a personal need of the poet, and by other poems as well. Poems are often implicit acts of comparison (sometimes in homage, sometimes in rivalry, most often in an uneasy combination of the two) to other poems and other poets. To train students to read poetry, therefore, entails, in part, to train them to read certain poems while keeping certain other poems in mind. Put simply, students really begin learning about poetry when most poems they read remind them in some way of some other poems they have read. I have tried to suggest affinities among selections in the anthology that will encourage fruitful and provocative cross-referencing of poems on the part of students.

All but a few of the lists are headed by a brief paragraph that offers some basic definitions of the issues or poetic features that the list highlights, and explains the rationale for the grouping, when it isn't obvious. These introductory paragraphs sketch some possible approaches to teaching the poems on the list, usually in the form of a series of related questions. In some cases, I imagine these might be most useful as questions you could pose for yourself in preparing a lesson; in other cases, you might wish to address these questions directly to the class in order to focus discussion, or you might use them as a basis for writing assignments. Sometimes these headnotes point to other lists that raise related issues. The point is to remind the instructor that it can be just as effective to teach elegies when asking the class to think about such matters as diction and closure as when explicitly considering questions of death and loss as poetic subjects. The implicit view behind such cross-references is that there are no purely formal issues in teaching poetry any more than there are purely thematic ones.

The bulk of this Course Guide is made up of questions that follow many of the individual poems in the lists. In general, these questions are designed to link each of the poems in specific ways to the concerns outlined in the headnote. Most of the questions are of the sort an instructor might address to undergraduates taking their first poetry course. I expect, though, that each instructor will find some of these questions more basic and pedagogically useful, but find others more suitable as guides to the teacher's own preparation than as inquiries for a class to explore. I hope that even those questions (and there are bound to be some) which some instructors find tendentious, picayune, or wrong-headed will be useful in helping them to come to clearer decisions about how best to teach the poems. (An instructor who poses one of the questions in this Guide that he or she judges least helpful and asks the class to consider why it is not a good question might well end up with a better lesson than would be sparked by a better question of my own.) The questions vary in focus, degree of specificity, and scope. Since, as I've said, a principal goal has been to help the instructor teach one poem in terms of others, "compare" is probably the most frequent suggestion in this Guide. Sometimes the questions try to suggest ways of thinking about the progression of the poem, how it moves from first line to last, how the opening stanzas prepare for the closing ones. For the most part I have tried to ask questions that will require the student to look carefully at the text, to read and reread, to gauge the effect of a particular word or line in terms of its relation to other parts of the poem, or even to other poems. Like other teachers, I have found that sweeping, vague questions can lead away from the poem at hand: "How does the speaker feel about all this?" or "What is the tone of this poem?" or "What is the poem about?" are less reliably effective questions than simpler, more specific ones which you would probably have to ask somewhere along the line anyway in guiding a class toward the larger answers. I prefer to ask, "How does this choice of word suggest what the speaker feels about all this?" or "What does the way this line is repeated tell us about the tone of this poem?" or even "What does the title of this poem suggest that it is about, and is the title accurate?" Such questions should have the initial effect, at least, of forcing students to read poems more slowly, and to treat these curious, patterned, unfamiliar structures of words with attention and patience.

From time to time the headnote suggests an exercise designed to teach the topic exemplified in the list. Some of these exercises involve revising parts of a poem to examine the effects of changes in certain poetic forms or devices; others involve imitating a poetic pattern or technique. Occasionally, brief suggestions for exercises in the teaching of an individual poem are listed with the questions for that poem, not in the headnote.

Page references are given to the Regular Edition first, then to the Shorter Edition (SE).

Dealing with Student Preconceptions

The lists, headnotes, and questions in this Guide offer very little in the way of historical or biographical information; the footnotes in the anthology itself provide most of the essential commentary of this nature. That the answers to most of the questions a beginning student is likely to be concerned with lie within the poems themselves (although that "within" demarcates a blurry borderline) seems to me one of the most important things a teacher can demonstrate in an introductory course in poetry. The goal of such a course should be to equip our students not as scholars but as readers of poetry. Beginning students, in my experience, can be all too eager to defer to some vague historical difference or to invent some esoteric authority to account for what seems to them the strangeness or subversiveness, the unfamiliar obliquity or uncomfortable bluntness of poems. If the opinion they take a poem to express about love, or old age, or religion, or loneliness does not concur with their own opinion or with what they take to be current opinions, many students will appeal to some principle of cultural or historical relativism: "That's the way they used to think about these things." One way for the instructor to keep from catering to this tendency is to take advantage of the freedom this anthology grants to teach poems from any period of English or American poetry in any sequence. Most of the lists in this guide try to suggest the pedagogic benefits of that freedom. You can help students to see the inadequacy of the notion that the difficulty of poetry lies chiefly in its outmoded dress and antiquated ways of thinking and feeling by having them discover that poems written ten years ago may be every bit as odd, bristly, and formidable as poems written four hundred years ago.

By these caveats I don't mean to imply, of course, that there are no differences in the challenges poems of different periods will present to students, or that they should be encouraged to ignore such differences. Even if, as Auden said, poetry makes nothing happen, it does not follow that nothing happens to poetry. The tendency of beginning students, however, to appeal to history as the sole, or at least primary, agent of the changes that make poetry hard to read is especially puzzling when you consider that if students have been told anything about poetry before they take up the subject in college, it is that poetry is timeless, inviolable, a separate realm in which "universal" human feelings find their expression. The historical range of the lists in this Guide should demonstrate that those supposedly universal feelings can take such different shapes and be sounded in such different tones that it is hard to be certain they are the same feelings at all.

Teaching poems by authors who belong to minority or ethnic groups or who for some other reason are placed outside of the group of white males whose modes of response are usually classed as "universal human feelings" is another way to combat the myth that poetry is an escape from history. By reading poems written by women, blacks, and other minority poets, students may observe another axis along which history works its changes. Here, as in all the modes of organizing a course suggested in this Guide, the instructor must navigate between the Scylla of overemphasizing the historical or cultural character of what poets are capable of saying and the Charybdis of exaggerating the continuities or uniformities of what poets say throughout history. "Not fare well, / But fare forward, voyagers."

1 VERSIFICATION

1.1 The Poetic Line

A. Illustrating the Variety of Poetic Lines

That poetry is written in lines is one of the most fundamental, but also one of the most complex, things about it. One good way of introducing this topic— and perhaps the course itself— would be to prepare a list illustrating the wide spectrum of possibilities for the poetic line that the anthology offers. The instructor might compile this list, or have students browse through the anthology, collecting samples of lines they find peculiar or interesting. Most students will recognize "I wandered lonely as a cloud," for instance (Wordsworth, p. 556; SE p. 290) as the kind of thing a line of poetry tends to sound like, but it is important that they realize that "'Were you happy?' 'Yes.' 'And are you still as happy?' 'Yes. And you?'" in Browning's "A Toccata of Galuppi's" (p. 730; SE p. 426) is also a line of poetry, as is "Six o'clock" in Eliot's "Preludes" (p. 997; SE p. 597) or "Methinks" in Thoreau's "I Am a Parcel of Vain Strivings Tied" (p. 752; SE p. 434). As a group, these poems and the one below suggest how wide and colorful is the spectrum of what poetic lines can look and sound like.

An allied exercise: select a few short prose paragraphs and have the students break them up into lines to make them look and sound as much like what they consider a poem (a free verse poem, most likely) to look and sound like, and explain the reasons for their choices. This is a useful exercise to do while studying end-stopped and enjambed lines as well (see Section 1.3).

Skelton, "To Mistress Margaret Hussey" (p. 67; SE p. 34): What is the effect of isolating in a line of its own each of the woman's praiseworthy attributes?
Gilbert, "When You're Lying Awake with a Dismal Headache" (p. 834; SE p. 487): What keeps these long lines from feeling long, compared, for example, to the longest lines in Lawrence's "Snake" or in any of the selections from Whitman? Why is the length of lines not simply a measure of how their printed words span across the page?
Williams, "Poem" (p. 946; SE p. 562) and "The Ivy Crown" (p. 950; SE p. 564): Why do these poems seem to be as much about the movement and force of William's lines as about a creeping cat ("Poem") or the dynamics of an enduring love ("The Ivy Crown")?

Lawrence, "Snake" (p. 592; SE p. 566): What sorts of energies are released when very short lines are set next to very long ones?

Auden, "In Praise of Limestone" (p. 1104; SE p. 670): Compare the effect of lines that seem to stand on their own ("They were right, my dear, all those voices were right," line 60), and lines that are a composite of logical or grammatical segments that started before them and continue after them ("Need to be altered.' (Intendant Caesars rose and," line 54). What kinds of interesting mistakes or incongruities will arise if you try to read such lines as a logical whole ("Remains incomprehensible: to become a pimp," line 40)?

Olson, "The Distances" (p. 1132; SE p. 689): Is this poem made up less of lines than of phrases? You might single out for discussion the little anecdote in lines 14-18: What is the effect of its strung-out appearance on the page? Why are the various bits of information that tell the story distributed in this way?

Bishop, "Jerónimo's House" (p. 1134; SE p. 690): How does the brevity of these lines help us to "come closer" to the house, as the speaker bids us (line 27)?

B. Lines of Varying Lengths

By beginning with a group of poems that feature lines of varying lengths, you can both illustrate the effect of such variations within a poem, and assign these poems as practice exercises in scansion. What is the effect of very short lines? How do short lines tend to isolate and emphasize the words in the line? How do longer lines bring attention to the grouping of words and sounds in the line? Even before you go into detail about the differences between metered verse and free verse, you might ask students about some general differences between the varied line lengths in poems with regular meter and poems in more open or "free" forms, comparing the last three poems on the list (Miles, Lowell, Baraka) with the rest of the list.

Donne, "Song" (p. 205; SE p. 100)
Herrick, "An Ode for Him" (p. 249; SE p. 131)
Herbert, "The Collar" (p. 262; SE p. 138)
Wordsworth, "Ode: Intimations of Immortality from Recollections of Early Childhood" (p. 551; SE p. 286)
Shelley, "To Jane: The Keen Stars Were Twinkling" (p. 639; SE p. 354)
Browning, "Home-Thoughts, From Abroad" (p. 720; SE p. 416)
Thoreau, "I Am a Parcel of Vain Strivings Tied" (p. 752; SE p. 434)
Hardy, "The Convergence of the Twain" (p. 848; SE p. 499)
Miles, "Midweek" (p. 1143; SE p. 698)

Lowell, "For the Union Dead" (p. 1198; SE p. 730)
Baraka, "In Memory of Radio" (p. 1356; SE p. 826)

1.2 Meter and Scansion

Scansion can become a tedious exercise— can seem to abandon the reading of poetry in favor of applying to it an arcane arithmetic— when it becomes a matter simply of identifying what meter a line or group of lines is written in. It is worth emphasizing the point that *lines* don't have meters, *poems* do.

Here is an exercise to heighten awareness of poetic rhythms and to demonstrate that it is often necessary to scan a line within the context of the entire poem in which it appears. The four-beat norm of ballads permits a varying number of unstressed syllables between strongly stressed syllables; this variation allows a four-beat line in an accentual meter to sound like a five-beat line in an accentual-syllabic meter. The line "For I crave one kiss of your clay-cold lips" in the ballad "The Unquiet Grave" (p. 75; SE p. 39) properly scans as a four-beat line in accentual or strong-stress meter (see "Versification," p. 1404; SE p. 856):

⏑ ⏑ / ⏑ / ⏑ ⏑ / ⏑ /
For I crave one kiss of your clay-cold lips,

And that is all I seek.

But if you insert this line into "Lycidas" (p. 275; SE p. 147)— it fits in rather nicely after line 14— it scans (technically, although it might not be read aloud as such) as iambic pentameter in an accentual-syllabic scheme ("Versification," p. 1405; SE p. 857), taking on the character of the lines surrounding it:

⏑ / ⏑ / ⏑ / ⏑ / ⏑ /
He must not float upon his watery bier

⏑ / ⏑ / ⏑ / ⏑ / ⏑ /
Unwept, and welter to the parching wind,

⏑ / ⏑ / ⏑ / ⏑ / ⏑ /
Without the meed of some melodious tear.

⏑ / | ⏑ / | ⏑ / | ⏑ / | ⏑ /
For I | crave one | kiss of | your clay | -cold lips.

While it makes sense to introduce metrical feet by adducing words or phrases that illustrate that foot (thus *alone* is an iamb, *lonely* a trochee, *loneliness* a dactyl, and *all alone* an anapest), it prevents some confusion, in teaching scansion, to demonstrate that any of these words can be used quite comfortably to conform to any meter. The presence of, say, the word *everything* in a line does not mean that the line must be dactylic. Although *everything* is a dactyl, a stressed syllable followed by two unstressed ones, it can fit perfectly into an iambic meter, in which its last syllable becomes stressed, like its first one: *everything*.

I include a list of poems that incorporate the dactylic word *everything*, in each of which it accommodates itself to other meters. Discussing in class the slight changes in emphasis and pronunciation that the word takes on in these examples is one way to train the ear for the rhythms of poetry. How does the word change in character in the anapests of "The Ruined Maid" and in the iambics of Webster, Wordsworth, and Frost? In different iambic poems, how does the word *everything* take on an altered emphasis and rhythm from the shadings of its metrical context?

O Melia, my dear, this does everything crown,
Who could have supposed I should meet you in Town?
        Hardy, "The Ruined Maid" (p. 847; SE p. 497)

Hark, now *everything* is still;
The Screech owl and the whistler shrill
Call upon our dame aloud.
        Webster, "Hark, Now Everything Is Still" (p. 241; SE p. 125)

The winds that will be howling at all hours,
And are upgathered now like sleeping flowers,
For this, for *everything*, we are out of tune...
        Wordsworth, "The World Is Too Much With Us"
        (p. 559; SE p. 292)

Where *everything* that meets the eye,
Flowers and grass and cloudless sky...
        Yeats, "Under Ben Bulben" (p. 895; SE p. 530)

When the word comes at the beginning of a line, as in the next two examples, how is its emphasis shaped by whether the preceding line is enjambed or end-stopped?

He thought that I was after him for a feather—
The white one in his tail; like one who takes
Everything said as personal to himself.
        Frost, "The Wood-Pile" (p. 912; SE p. 540)

Your absence has gone through me
Like thread through a needle.
Everything I do is stitched with its color.
        Merwin, "Separation" (p. 1296; SE p. 790)

A. Dimeter ("Versification," p. 1407; SE p. 859)

Jonson, "A Hymn to God the Father" (p. 231; SE p. 120)
Blake, "The Sick Rose" (p. 505; SE p. 263)

B. Trimeter ("Versification," p. 1407; SE p. 859)

Ralegh, "The Lie" (p. 107; SE p. 60)
Campion, "Now Winter Nights Enlarge" (p. 200; SE p. 96)
Nashe, "A Litany in Time of Plague" (p. 202; SE p. 98)
MacNeice, "London Rain" (p. 1114; SE p. 677)
Roethke, "My Papa's Waltz" (p. 1117; SE p. 679)

C. Tetrameter ("Versification," p. 1407; SE p. 859)

The four-beat line is common in ballads, hymns, and songs. But it
proves serviceable as well for epitaphs (Wotton, Jonson, Johnson),
religious poetry (Vaughan), for wittily erotic verse (Donne,
Herrick, Suckling, Marvell), and meditative verse, where a voice
contemplates the state of its own consciousness (Milton, Bradstreet, Wordsworth). In the modern era tetrameter can be used to
allude to the ballad or other traditions of popular verse (Cummings,
Eliot, Gunn).

Anonymous, "The Twa Corbies" (p. 74; SE p. 37)
Anonymous, "There Is a Lady Sweet and Kind" (p. 88; SE p. 48)
Wyatt, "My Lute, Awake!" (p. 92; SE p. 51)
Ralegh, "The Nymph's Reply to the Shepherd" (p. 105; SE p. 58)
Campion, "When to Her Lute Corinna Sings" (p. 199; SE p. 95) and
    "There Is a Garden in Her Face" (p. 201; SE p. 97)
Wotton, "On His Mistress, the Queen of Bohemia" (p. 203; SE
    p. 99)
Donne, "The Ecstasy" (p. 213; SE p. 106)
Jonson, "On My First Daughter" (p. 224; SE p. 114), "Epitaph on
    Elizabeth, L.H." (p. 228; SE p. 117), and "Queen and
    Huntress" (p. 237; SE p. 121)
Herrick, "The Vine" (p. 242; SE p. 126) and "To His Conscience"
    (p. 250; SE p. 132)
Carew, "A Song" (p. 269; SE p. 143)
Milton, "L'Allegro" (p. 284; SE p. 156) and "Il Penseroso" (p. 287;
    SE p. 159). The tetrameters take over at line 11 in each
    poem; what has to be banished before this meter can be
    established?
Suckling, "Upon My Lady Carlisle's Walking in Hampton Court
    Garden" (p. 318; SE p. 166)
Bradstreet, "Here Follows Some Verses Upon the Burning of Our
    House July 10th, 1666" (p. 325; SE p. 170)
Marvell, "Bermudas" (p. 336; SE p. 177), and all other Marvell
    selections except "The Fair Singer"
Vaughan, "The Retreat" (p. 350; SE p. 185)
Johnson, "On the Death of Dr. Robert Levet" (p. 458; SE p. 246)
Blake, from Poetical Sketches, "Song" (p. 496; SE p. 258) and
    from Songs of Innocence, "Introduction" (p. 497; SE p. 259)
Wordsworth, "I Wandered Lonely as a Cloud" (p. 556; SE p. 290)

Emerson, "Concord Hymn" (p. 665; SE p. 375)
Tennyson, "Mariana" (p. 698; SE p. 396). The first eight lines of
    each stanza are in tetrameter: what is the effect of the shift into
    ballad stanza (alternating tetrameter and trimeter lines) in the
    refrain?
Yeats, "Under Ben Bulben" (p. 895; SE p. 530)
Dunbar, "We Wear the Mask" (p. 904; SE p. 537)
Frost, "Provide, Provide" (p. 921; SE p. 545)
Eliot, "Sweeney Among the Nightingales" (p. 999; SE p. 598)
Cummings, "my father moved through dooms of love" (p. 1045; SE
    p. 632)
Wilbur, "Museum Piece" (p. 1221, SE p. 745)
Snodgrass, "April Inventory" (p. 1287; SE p. 783)
Gunn, "Street Song" (p. 1305; SE p. 795)

D. Iambic Pentameter ("Versification," p. 1407; SE p. 859)

A large proportion of poems in English, and hence a large proportion of poems in this anthology, are in iambic pentameter. The list
for this section includes only a small portion of the anthology's
selections that might be used to illustrate the development of the
pentameter from the fourteenth century to the twentieth; it includes poems that are in iambic pentameter, but are in none of the
pentameter forms that are listed separately below: free verse (1.5),
heroic couplets (2.2), and sonnets (3.2). What changes can you
detect in the meter's rigor or tautness, from the bouncing, chiefly
end-stopped couplets of Chaucer, to the colloquial, slackened lines of
Frost or Lowell?

Chaucer, from The Canterbury Tales, "The Pardoner's Prologue and
    Tale" (p. 24; SE p. 6): The Epilogue (lines 631-68) is parti-
    cularly good for illustrating the flexibility of Chaucer's
    pentameters. How does Chaucer make the pentameter line
    serve for the Pardoner's slimy sales pitch (lines 631-57), the
    Host's invective (lines 657-68), the Knight's call for recon-
    ciliation (lines 670-79), and the narrator's exposition (lines
    668-69, 672, and 680)?
Wyatt, "Mine Own John Poins" (p. 95; SE p. 52)
Surrey, "Wyatt Resteth Here" (p. 98; SE p. 55)
Tichborne, "Tichborne's Elegy" (p. 105; SE p. 58)
Spenser, from The Faerie Queene, Book V, Canto II (p. 131; SE
    p. 62): How does the final hexameter (six-foot line) of the
    Spenserian stanza make the prevailing five-foot line more
    audible? Compare Shelley's use of this stanza in his elegy for
    Keats, "Adonais" (p. 626; SE p. 343), and to Keats's adaptation
    of the Spenserian stanza to a different kind of storytelling in
    "The Eve of St. Agnes" (p. 650; SE p. 360).
Campion, "My Sweetest Lesbia" (p. 198; SE p. 95)

Donne, "The Good-Morrow" (p. 204; SE p. 100) and "Elegy VII" (p. 216; SE p. 109)

Jonson, "Inviting a Friend to Supper" (p. 226; SE p. 116) and "To Penshurst" (p. 228; SE p. 119)

Herrick, "The Argument of His Book" (p. 242; SE p. 125)

Milton, "On Shakespeare" (p. 291; SE p. 163)

Bradstreet, "The Author to Her Book" (p. 324; SE p. 169)

Marvell, "The Fair Singer" (p. 340; SE p. 181)

Taylor, "Meditation 8" (p. 381; SE p. 197)

Gray, "Elegy Written in a Country Churchyard" (p. 463; SE p. 248)

Wordsworth, "Elegaic Stanzas" (p. 558; SE p. 290)

Landor, "Dying Speech of an Old Philosopher" (p. 587, SE p. 318)

Wordsworth, "Ode: Intimations of Immortality" (p. 551; SE p. 286): Iambic pentameter lines are interwoven with shorter lines in the varied stanza forms of this ode. Compare the stanzas that end with pentameter lines (4, 5, 6, 8, and 11) with those that do not: how does iambic pentameter become associated with some form of stability or permanence? Why does pentameter become the dominant meter in the final stanza?

Shelley, "Ode to the West Wind" (p. 620; SE p. 337): Compare the use of pentameter throughout this ode (written in terza rima) to its occasional use in Wordworth's "Ode: Intimations of Immortality" (p. 551; SE p. 286).

Emerson, "The Rhodora" (p. 666; SE p. 375)

Tennyson, Songs from *The Princess*, "Tears, Idle Tears" and "Now Sleeps the Crimson Petal" (p. 705; SE p. 404)

Arnold, "The Scholar-Gypsy" (p. 783; SE p. 458): What is the effect of the trimeter lines around which these otherwise pentameter stanzas pivot?

Meredith, from *Modern Love*, 48 ("Their sense is with their senses all mixed in") (p. 801; SE p. 469)

Morris, "The Earthly Paradise" (p. 832; SE p. 485)

Yeats, "Adam's Curse" (p. 879; SE p. 516) and "The Second Coming" (p. 883; SE p. 520)

Robinson, "Richard Cory" (p. 899; SE p. 533)

Frost, "The Most of It" (p. 423; SE p. 546) and "The Gift Outright" (p. 923; SE p. 547): See "Versification," p. 1408, SE p. 860 for a scansion of "The Gift Outright."

Stevens, "To the One of Fictive Music" (p. 932; SE p. 554)

Pound, "Portrait d'une Femme" (p. 959; SE p. 572)

Owen, "Strange Meeting" (p. 1035; SE p. 624)

Bogan, "Song for the Last Act" (p. 1053; SE p. 638)

Crane, "Royal Palm" (p. 1059; SE p. 644)

Hope, "Australia" (p. 1108; SE p. 672)

Klein, "Indian Reservation: Caughnawaga" (p. 1124; SE p. 684)

Lowell, "The Quaker Graveyard in Nantucket" (p. 1185; SE p. 720): How do the occasional shorter lines help to bring out the cadence of the pentameters?

Nemerov, "The Historical Judas" (p. 1218; SE p. 743)

Wilbur, "Boy at the Window" (p. 1222; SE p. 746)

Hecht, "The Feast of Stephen" (p. 1238; SE p. 756)
Merrill, "The Victor Dog" (p. 1282; SE p. 780)
Gunn, "On the Move" (p. 1301; SE p. 792)

E. Blank Verse— and Everday English

The selections listed below from Wordsworth, Tennyson, Browning, and Frost, among others, raise the vexed question of whether unrhymed iambic pentameter is in fact close to "the natural rhythms of spoken English," as Jon Stallworthy suggests in the "Versification" essay (p. 1413; SE p. 865). Is it merely convention (for instance, its long history in dramatic verse) that seems to make blank verse so suitable for creating a meditative or speaking voice, or is it this meter's reflection of or adaptation to English rhythms and intonations that fosters the impression that an individual voice is speaking, with its unrehearsed hesitations, its spontaneous questions, and its unfolding qualifications?

An exercise that may bring this debate alive is to have students listen to spoken English for a week (to conversations, lectures, news broadcasts, etc.) and try to detect passages or lines that approximate iambic pentameter ("I can't believe I have a test today." "Let's leave that topic for tomorrow's class." "The Congressman could not be reached for comment"). Have them submit two or three such overheard pentameters (or perhaps bits of colloquial conversation as represented in a novel or play) along with two or three they have made up; the point is to make the invented lines sound as if they have overheard them, and see if the class can tell the difference. Or have the students compile all the lines submitted by the class and arrange them to make a dramatic monologue out of them.

Another exercise: Have students recast into iambic pentameter a short poem in another meter. How does the speaker's tone change with this transformation? For instance, expanding the clipped lines of Dickinson's Poem 49, "I never lost as much but twice" (p. 804; SE p. 472) turns the poem into more of a sober, meditative account of loss than a riddling cry of pain, and requires the reviser to fill out with adjectives the curt, epigrammatic phrases ("door of God"); perhaps Emily Brontë (see "Remembrance," (p. 754; SE p. 435), but never Emily Dickinson, could have written this version (my additions or changes are bracketed):

> I never lost as much, [except for] twice,
> And that was in the [unforgiving] sod.
> Twice have I stood, a beggar, [all in rags],
> Before the [shut, unyielding] door of God.

See also the suggestions in the next list of poems under "Variations on Blank Verse" for a similar exercise on Whitman's "When I Heard the Learn'd Astronomer" (p. 764; SE p. 441).

Poems in blank verse that aspire to a conversational informality and naturalness include:

Wordsworth, from *The Prelude* (p. 538; SE p. 276)
Coleridge, "Frost at Midnight" (p. 566; SE p. 297)
Frost, "Mending Wall" (p. 908; SE p. 539), "The Wood-pile
    (p. 912; SE p. 540), "Birches" (p. 914; SE p. 541),
    "West-Running Brook," (p. 918; SE p. 543), "Directive"
    (p. 924; SE p. 547)
Lowell, "1930's" (p. 1199; SE p. 732)

F. Variations on Blank Verse

To what subjects does unrhymed iambic pentameter seem best suited? How does the absence of rhyme put pressure on other formal features (syntax, enjambment, repetition, rhetorical structures) to do the job of annotating words (defining, qualifying, linking to other instances of the word and other words in the poem)? Or of associating words and units of thought in the way that rhyme associates them in other pentameter poems, such as in heroic couplets? How do the looser five-beat forms of twentieth-century poetry (Stevens, Lowell) allude to the blank verse tradition even while deviating from it?

Milton, *Paradise Lost*, Book I, lines 1-26 (p. 295; SE p. 165): Freeing
    his poetry from what he called "the troublesome and modern
    bondage of rhyming," Milton arrived at what to Samuel Johnson
    seemed "verse only to the eye." What did Johnson mean, and
    was he right?
Blake, "To the Evening Star" (p. 497; SE p. 259): Set against
    conventional sonnets, this blank verse sonnet is a good poem in
    which to test what happens when rhyme is omitted from a verse
    genre that is normally rhymed.
Wordsworth, "Lines Composed a Few Miles above Tintern Abbey" (p.
    523; SE p. 273) and selection from *The Prelude*, Book I (p. 538;
    SE p. 276)
Coleridge, "Frost at Midnight" (p. 566; SE p. 297)
Emerson, "Hamatreya" (p. 669; SE p. 376): The frame (lines 1-27) is
    in blank verse, while the "Earth-song" it introduces is in a
    ragged dimeter. The shift from blank verse to a rhymed and
    strongly cadenced two-beat metric invites us to ask why the
    earth cannot speak in blank verse, too. Is blank verse inappro-
    priate for a song? Is the speaker of the last four lines (lines
    60-63) the same as the speaker of the opening meditation?
    Why doesn't this poem return to blank verse after the song?
Tennyson, "Ulysses" (p. 704; SE p. 402) and "Tithonus" (p. 713; SE
    p. 411): How does Tennyson make these two mythical
    figures— one heroically yearning, the other eternally weary—
    sound quite different although they speak in the same meter?

Browning, "Fra Lippo Lippi" (p. 723; SE p. 419): What is the
metrical effect of the snatches of song Fra Lippo interjects? By
interposing moments of strongly stressed rhythm, do they
encourage our belief that Fra Lippo's speech is natural and
spontaneous, rather than designed to seem so through skillful
manipulation of meter?

Whitman, "When I Heard the Learn'd Astronomer" (p. 764; SE
p. 441): A poem not in blank verse but useful for teaching it: why
does the last line fall into iambic pentameter? The meditative
tone and the way some of Whitman's lines flirt with the five-beat
tradition make this poem a good basis for a versification
exercise: have students rewrite this poem as blank verse and
account for what happens. For instance, recasting the first line
as

> When once I heard the learn'd astronomer

brings out all four syllables of the last word with a clarity much
greater than in Whitman's line. Arguably it also underlines the
word's etymology (*astron,* star + *nomos,* law) as the more
blurred, vernacular pronunciation of Whitman's line does not.
Which of Whitman's extravagances become pruned by rewriting
the poem in blank verse? How does his voice, and the very
nature of his protest here, change when it speaks in iambic
pentameter? (An even more revealing assignment for ad-
vanced students, as much about poetic voice as about meter:
rewrite "When I Heard the Learn'd Astronomer" in blank verse
as Wordsworth, Browning, and Frost would have done it.)

Frost, "West-running Brook" (p. 919; SE p. 543): Does the way the
husband and wife share a pentameter line between them figure,
and enhance our sense of, their reciprocity? Or does it point to
one person's power over the other? Which member of the
couple tends to establish a line, and which to complete it? In
the opening line, how does Frost use the blank verse context to
give his speakers a distinctive intonation? The word "north"
appears three times in the first line: what gives it a different
inflection each time? A line like 37 might seem convincing
evidence that we actually do speak in a rough blank verse all the
time; what it exemplifies, however, is the immense skill with
which Frost makes the meter sound conversational, as he does
also in "Mending Wall" (p. 908; SE p. 539), "The Wood-Pile"
(p. 912; SE p. 540), and "Birches" (p. 914; SE p. 541).

Stevens, "Sunday Morning" (p. 929; SE p. 551)

Eliot, "The Dry Salvages" (p. 1013; SE p. 611): Not in blank verse,
but an iambic pentameter surfaces in interesting ways from time
to time; having students spot what they think are iambic
pentameter lines in section 5 (lines 184-215 in particular) is a
good way to raise questions about the degree to which the

metrical context of a line determines how we should scan it. See Section 1.1 for more on this.

Jarrell, "Well Water" (p. 1171; SE p. 710): Another poem that weaves in and out of an iambic pattern; as in Whitman's "When I Heard the Learn'd Astronomer," does the more pronounced iambic regularity of the last line add to the solidity of the poem's closure? Does it also provide a norm against which the other lines' deviations from iambic pentameter can be heard?

Lowell, "1930's" (p. 1199; SE p. 732)

G. Hexameter ("Versification," p. 1407; SE p. 859)

Poems written wholly in iambic hexameter are rare (two notable examples, listed below, are by Sidney and Dowson); the hexameter line, or alexandrine, is more often used to lend solidity or stability at the end of a stanza written in a shorter measure. The closing alexandrine has varying functions in the Spenserian stanza of *The Faerie Queene* (p. 110; SE p. 62), and in its adaptations in English Romantic poetry, notably Shelley's "Adonais" (p. 626; SE p. 343) and Keats's "The Eve of St. Agnes" (p. 650; SE p. 360). Spenser uses the hexameter close also for the resonant refrain of "Epithalamion" (p. 138; SE p. 68). Partly in order to forge a link between his poetry and Spenser's, Milton ends the stanzas of "On the Morning of Christ's Nativity" (p. 279; SE p. 151) with an alexandrine. Heroic couplets are sometimes varied by the occasional alexandrine, as in Dryden's "To the Memory of Mr. Oldham" (p. 374; SE p. 192).

Spenser, from *The Faerie Queene*, Book V, Canto II, stanzas 29-50 (p. 110; SE p. 62) and "Epithalamion" (p. 138; SE p. 68): Ask students to categorize the various ways Spenser uses the alexandrine to bring the stanza to a close; for example, to undercut the stanza's (here, the Gyant's) claims (44, 48) to summarize the stanza with a maxim or nugget of truth (stanzas 40, 41, 43, 45), or to carry the story forward (33, 49).

Sidney, from *Astrophel and Stella*, 1 ("Loving in truth, and fain in verse my love to show") (p. 156; SE p. 80)

Milton, "On the Morning of Christ's Nativity" (p. 279; SE p. 151)

Dryden, "To the Memory of Mr. Oldham" (p. 374; SE p. 192)

Swift, "A Description of a City Shower" (p. 382; SE p. 206): In this poem written in heroic couplets, what is the effect of the final hexameter line? How does it help to suggest the amount of assorted refuse that the flood collects?

Shelley, "Adonais" (p. 626; SE p. 343)

Keats, "The Eve of St. Agnes" (p. 650; SE p. 360)

Hardy, "The Convergence of the Twain" (p. 848; SE p. 499)

Dowson, "Non sum qualis eram bonae sub regno Cynarae" (p. 898; SE p. 532)

H. Meters Other Than Iambic ("Versification," pp. 1405-07; SE pp. 857-58)

Since by far the major portion of poems in English, and hence in this anthology, are in some form of iambic meter, it is most sensible, I think, to teach as a unit all other poetic feet—trochaic, anapestic, and dactylic. This list includes as well iambic poems with lines or moments that are markedly non-iambic.

[Trochaic]
Blake, "The Tyger" (p. 505; SE p. 264)
Tennyson, "Frater, Ave Atque Vale" (p. 716; SE p. 412)
Graves, "Warning to Children" (p. 1050; SE p. 635)
[Anapestic]
Montagu, "The Lover: A Ballad" (p. 441; SE p. 237)
Swinburne, "A Forsaken Garden" (p. 842; SE p. 493)
Hardy, "The Ruined Maid" (p. 847; SE p. 497)
Page, "The Stenographers" (p. 1203; SE p. 735)
[Dactylic]
Hardy, "The Voice" (p. 850; SE p. 501)

1.3 Enjambment and End-stopped Lines ("Versification," p. 1409; SE p. 861)

The lists below isolate poems in which either enjambment or end-stopping is dominant. Most poems will combine these two sorts of lineation, sometimes in ways that respond closely to the poem's content. In Keats's "On First Looking into Chapman's Homer" (p. 648; SE p. 359), for instance, the first eight lines, corresponding to the period before the poet read Homer in Chapman's translation, are end-stopped; the eye-opening experience of reading Chapman releases the poem into a more fluid pattern of enjambment.

An exercise to clarify the difference between enjambed and end-stopped lines: Choose one of the poems from the list of end-stopped lines, revise it by breaking it up into shorter lines with strong enjambments, and ask students to discuss the changes in meaning and emphasis that result. For instance, relineate Smart's "For I will consider my Cat Jeoffrey" (p. 470; SE p. 253) as Williams might have written it, so that lines 749-50 become something like this:

> For he can jump
> over a stick,
>
> which is patience
> upon proof
> positive. For he

can spraggle upon
waggle at the word
of command.

A. Enjambment

In strongly enjambed lines, the meaning of the line changes,
sometimes just slightly, sometimes greatly, when the reader
discovers the syntactic continuation of the line in the next one.
For instance, in Blake's "To the Evening Star" (p. 497; SE p. 259),
line 8 ends with the injunction to the star to "Let thy west wind
sleep on"; line 9 reveals that "sleep on" here is not an idiomatic
phrase meaning "continue to sleep, keep on sleeping," but rather
requires completion by an object for the preposition "on": "sleep
on / The lake." The use of enjambment requires continual
readjustments of pattern and expectation in a poem like Crase's
"Summer." In a first reading of lines 10-12, for instance,

> Our momentum is still an adjunct
> Of the year and the territory we cover
> Is legitimately ours . . . ,

we are likely to take both items in line 11 as going with "adjunct"
in line 10, but proceeding to the next line reveals that the second
item in line 11, "the territory we cover," is governed by "Is
legitimately ours" in line 12. It is not that our going on to the next
line reveals the correct reading of the run-on line, but that both
meanings of the line hover in suspension. A strong enjambment
may make a single word straddle two lines, momentarily isolating
the elements that make up the word, as in Herrick's "The Lily in a
Crystal" (p. 245; SE p. 128, lines 25-26), Williams's "The Red
Wheelbarrow," or Creeley's "Heroes" (p. 1271; SE p. 776, lines
12-13). A run-on line may leap across a stanza break, as throughout
Tate's "The Lost Pilot" (p. 1391; SE p. 846). In the poems listed
here the enjambments are particularly strong or noticeable, or
especially important to the poem's tone and meaning.
    An exercise: have students relineate parts of poems from this
list to eliminate as many ambiguities or possible confusions as they
can, which may mean making the lines as end-stopped as possible.
What new meanings and openings for interpretation does this
rearrangment introduce into the poem?

Milton, from *Paradise Lost*, Book I [The Invocation] (p. 295; SE
    p. 165)
Blake, "To the Evening Star" (p. 497; SE p. 259): Ending a line
    with "the," as Blake does line 5, is a rarity in poetry before the
    modern period; compare the effect of this line break here and

in such later instances listed below as Rich's "The Ninth
Symphony of Beethoven Understood at Last as a Sexual
Message" (line 13) and Snyder's "Above Pate Valley" (line 12),
and in other poems as well, such as Merrill's "Whitebeard on
Videotape" (p. 1283; SE p. 781, line 5), Walcott"s "Europa"
(p. 1338; SE p. 814, lines 1 and 13), and Ondaatje's "Burning
Hills" (p. 1389; SE p. 844, line 18).

Browning, "My Last Duchess" (p. 717; SE p. 413): What features of
the Duke's language make it flow so naturally from one line to
the next that it is almost impossible to hear that the poem is
written in rhymed couplets?

Robinson, "Miniver Cheevy" (p. 900; SE p. 533)

Williams, "The Red Wheelbarrow" (p. 945; SE p. 561) and "Poem"
(p. 946; SE p. 562)

Brooks, "We Real Cool" (p. 1183; SE p. 719)

Merrill, "Upon a Second Marriage" (p. 1280; SE p. 779)

Rich, "The Ninth Symphony of Beethoven Understood at Last as a
Sexual Message" (p. 1317; SE p. 800)

Crase, "Summer" (p. 1395; SE p. 848)

B. End-stopped Lines

End-stopping is a different sort of achievement in the selections
from Smart, Whitman, Ginsberg, Koch, and Corso; without a
metrical count to adhere to, these poets can extend their lines
as long as they want to, or as long as the line needs to be to complete its unit of thought. How do Smart and Whitman both try to
imitate, and thus allude to, the feel of Biblical poetry? How do the
extended, end-stopped lines of Ginsberg and Corso allude to
Whitman?

Tichborne, "Tichborne's Elegy" (p. 105; SE p. 58)

Smart, from *Jubilate Agno* ("For I will consider my Cat Jeoffrey")
(p. 470; SE p. 253)

Whitman, "Vigil Strange I Kept on the Field One Night" (p. 768;
SE p. 445): All of the selections from Whitman are good
examples of end-stopped poetry. How does Whitman's end-
stopping serve his needs as a list-maker, as a poet who tries to
get the whole world into his poetry?

Koch, "You Were Wearing" (p. 1251; SE p. 763)

Ginsberg, "In the Baggage Room at Greyhound" (p. 1278; SE
p. 776)

Corso, "Marriage" (p. 1321; SE p. 804): Although there is often no
punctuation mark at the end of the lines, each completes a
single unit of thought or completes a single item in a list.

1.4 Rhyme ("Versification," pp. 1410-12; SE pp. 862-64)

One way to introduce students to rhyme is to adduce poems whose uses of rhyme are also implicit arguments about rhyme, such as Dryden's "Ode for St. Cecilia's Day" and Keats's "On the Sonnet." The question, for example, of whether rhyme is a fettering or freeing device of poetry is debated within some poems themselves. Thus for Dryden rhyme represents or corresponds to a divine harmony, whereas for Keats rhyme is a cruel manacling of the muse. Rhyme sometimes sounds a dangerous lulling chime in Poe and Tennyson. Lear and Blake remind us, by the effect of their exact echoing, that we ordinarily expect rhyme words to sound a little different as well as the same. In defending rhyme against the charge of mere jingle, it is useful to ask students to look at particular pairs of rhymed words and to consider which ones are predictable or conventional (moon-soon; bowers-flowers) and which startling, in that they bring together words from utterly different realms of thought or discourse (saint-paint; gunnery-nunnery). Writers of light verse are fond of such unlikely pairings; writers of satirical verse may sharpen their barbs by expressively shifting between conventional and startling rhymes (Blake, Pope). Another way to defend rhyme against jingle is to use imperfect rhyme of various kinds.

Herrick, "To the Virgins, to Make Much of Time" (p. 246; SE p. 129): Almost a compendium of the *carpe diem* devices of seduction poetry (see 7.16.A), this poem seems as inevitable in its rhyming as its seductions, which makes it a good poem to teach the force of conventional rhyming. An exercise: before having students read this poem, give them the title, and the first (or, where easier, second) word in each of the poem's rhymes; see if the class can come up with the completing rhymes. In a seduction poem, "marry" goes with "tarry" (as it also does, delightfully, in Lear's "The Owl and the Pussy-Cat," (p. 750; SE p. 433) just as surely as "sun" will lead to some version of "run" (as it does at the end of Marvell's "To His Coy Mistress," p. 337; SE p. 178).

Dryden, "A Song for St. Cecilia's Day" (p. 375; SE p. 193): Like most irregular odes, this one is good for teaching rhyme scheme, since the pattern differs in each stanza. How does the first stanza suggest that divine harmony is a kind of cosmic rhyme? Why is the first appearance of exact end rhyme delayed until line 7, with the words "Arise ye, more than dead"? (As the chaotic atoms become ordered, so does the rhyme scheme. The divine fiat is almost, here, "Let there be rhyme.")

Pope, "The Rape of the Lock" (p. 409; SE p. 211): You can dip in almost anywhere and find many instances of witty rhyming. Often Pope pairs rhymed words with the force of *zeugma*: that is, the principle of pairing the serious and the trivial within a single line, often through making two unlike sounds the object of the same verb— "Or stain her honor or her new brocade" (Canto II, line 107). A similar effect is found within a pair of lines through rhyme, such as in "One speaks the glory of the British Queen, / And one describes a charming Indian screen" (Canto III, lines 13-14). What sorts of variety and surprise does Pope achieve by rarely rhyming two words that function as the same part of speech? For instance, in "Unnumbered throngs on every side are seen / Of bodies changed to various forms by Spleen," (Canto IV, lines 47-48), a verb (seen) rhymes with a noun (Spleen), whereas the "Queen-screen" couplet (another rhyme on the *een* sound) pairs two incongruous nouns, and pairs them in a deflating or descending order. (For another comic rhyme on "Queen," see Canto IV, lines 57-58.)

Blake, "The Garden of Love" (p. 506; SE p. 265) and "A Question Answered" (p. 508; SE p. 266): How does the shift to markedly audible internal rhymes in the last two lines signal the unnatural binding of love by the priests? In "A Question Answered," how does rhyming the same line suggest a bitter refusal of witty antithesis? How does Blake undercut our expectations— established by the witty wars of the sexes in poets like Pope and Swift— to have the second question answered with something like, "A pocket lined to buy them rich attire"? Compare the comic effect of Lear's use of this device of rhyming a line with the same line.

Byron, "So We'll Go No More A-Roving" (p. 592; SE p. 321): How does this poem's grace derive in some measure from the utter conventionality of its rhymes (night-bright; soon-moon)? (For a compelling answer, have students listen to Joan Baez singing this poem to Richard Dyer-Bennet's setting on the album *Baez 5.*)

Keats, "On the Sonnet" (p. 657; SE p. 368): How does Keats's rhyme scheme loosen the muse's "garlands"? Compare to the rhyme schemes of other sonnets.

Poe, "The City in the Sea" (p. 695; SE p. 394)

Tennyson, "The Lotos-Eaters" (p. 700; SE p. 398): How does the opening of the poem suggest that the effect of rhyming a word with itself will not always be comical? How does the accumulation of lulling rhymes point toward the sailors' drug-deadened wish for changelessness?

Lear, "There Was an Old Man with a Beard" and "There Was an Old Man in a Tree" (p. 750; SE p. 433): What is humorous about the flat rhyming of the same word at the end of the first and fourth lines? Have students make up a different last line with a different rhyme-word and discuss the effects of this change.

Gilbert, "I Am the Very Model of a Modern Major-General" (p. 833; SE p. 486): This patter song is an extravaganza of feminine rhymes ("Versification," p. 1412; SE p. 864). How does the heterogeneity of the words paired in these couplets figure the miscellaneous trivia a British commander had to know, instead of knowing how to command?

Swinburne, "The Garden of Proserpine" (p. 839; SE p. 491): Why does the combination of trimeter lines (where you don't have to wait long for the rhyme to hit the ear) and each stanza's little crescendo of a triplet with feminine rhymes make the rhyme in this poem very audible? Take one stanza and add one foot to each line, then two feet: how is the effect of the rhyme changed?

Thomas, "In My Craft of Sullen Art" (p. 1181; SE p. 718): How many lines may intervene between two words before their rhyme is no longer detectable? Is "art" in line 1 too far removed from "heart" in line 11 for us to hear them as a rhyming pair? Do the intervening off-rhymes to "art" and "heart"—"night" and "arms"—preserve or confuse our memory of the initial rhyme-word, "art," until its paired sound reaches our ear at the end of the stanza?

Snodgrass, "April Inventory" (p. 1287; SE p. 783): What is the effect of the comic rhymes, almost worthy of Ogden Nash, that end several of the stanzas?

A. Internal Rhyme ("Versification," p. 1411; SE p. 863)

What are the diverse effects of internal rhyming? Compare the celebratory or capering lilt it gives to the poems by Nash and Lear to the somber, elegaic note it strikes in the poems by Coleridge, Poe, and Tennyson.

Nashe, "Spring, the Sweet Spring" (p. 201; SE p. 97)

Blake, "The Garden of Love" (p. 506; SE p. 265): What is the effect of the introduction of internal rhyme in the last two lines?

Coleridge, "The Rime of the Ancient Mariner" (p. 567; SE p. 298): What is the effect of the occasional use of internal rhyme, as in lines 7, 22, 27, 31, and so on? Does the frequency of internal rhyme seem to respond to the tone or events of the poem?

Poe, "Annabel Lee" (p. 697; SE p. 395): What is the effect of the increasing use of internal rhyme in the final stanza?

Tennyson, "The Splendor Falls" (p. 705; SE p. 403)

Lear, "The Owl and the Pussy-Cat" (p. 750; SE p. 433)

Gilbert, "When You're Lying Awake with a Dismal Headache" (p. 834; SE p. 487)

Hopkins, "God's Grandeur" (p. 855; SE p. 502)

B. Imperfect Rhyme ("Versification," p. 1412; SE p. 864)

Dickinson, Poem 465 "I Heard a Fly buzz—when I died—" (p. 809; SE p. 476): Off-rhyme allows "Room" to rhyme with both "Storm" and "Firm." Note that, as in a number of Dickinson's poems, the rhyme becomes perfect in the last stanza (the poem begins with the slant rhyme "be-fly" and ends with the exact rhyme "me-see"): does this progression give the poem a surer finality? In Poem 712, "Because I could not stop for Death" (p. 812; SE p. 476), what is the effect of the mixture of perfect and imperfect rhyme? Dickinson's first editors changed line 20 to "The Cornice but a mound": Why did they think this would be an improvemnt? Is it?

Yeats, "The Scholars" (p. 881; SE p. 518): How does the perfect rhyme of the second stanza figure the mechanical conformity of the old scholars? Do the first stanza's off-rhymes correspond to the ardent creativity of the young poets? Compare to Blake's "The Garden of Love" for a similar effect.

Owen, "Strange Meeting" (p. 1035; SE p. 624): Is the unsettling effect of Owen's couplets in pararhyme (see "Versification," p. 1412; SE p. 864) undercut by its predictability? Compare with other couplet poems with perfect rhyme.

Stafford, "Traveling through the Dark" (p. 1174; SE p. 712)

Thomas, "The Hunchback in the Park" (p. 1178; SE p. 715)

Lowell, "Skunk Hour" (p. 1195; SE p. 728)

Hughes, "The Thought-Fox" (p. 1323; SE p. 806)

1.5 Free Verse (Unmetered Verse) ("Versification," pp. 1420-22; SE pp. 872-74)

Which of these examples of free verse seem to have taken their cue from Whitman, allowing the line to spill its length along the page until the sentence it utters is finished? Which seem rather to be free verse for the typewriter, in the tradition of Williams, imposing a rough rule of an approximate number of characters per line? What range of effects does the ragged left-hand margin have?

What principles may govern the line-breaks in free verse? Which poets tend to use line-ends to close a syntactic phrase, and which use line-ends to break or suspend a syntactic phrase? What different kinds of signals for reading the poem aloud are suggested in these diverse styles of free verse?

Whitman, from *Song of Myself* (p. 760; SE p. 438)

Williams, "The Ivy Crown" (p. 950; SE p. 564)

Lawrence, "Bavarian Gentians" (p. 956; SE p. 568): The first line is iambic pentameter, but thereafter lines expand. You might note that Lawrence's meter is free, but that his diction can be quite conventional or even "high," as in the inversion of "arms Plutonic." (On Diction, see Section 5.5.)

H.D., "Wine Bowl" (p. 980; SE p. 586)

Jeffers, "Birds and Fishes" (p. 985; SE p. 589)

Eliot, "The Love Song of J. Alfred Prufrock" (p. 994; SE p. 594); from *Four Quartets*, "The Dry Salvages" (p. 1013; SE p. 611)

Warren, "Where the Slow Fig's Purple Sloth" (p. 1089; SE p. 661)

Roethke, "The Far Field" (p. 1121; SE p. 681): What is the effect of the increasingly stable pentameter rhythms of the final section?

Olson, "The Distances" (p. 1132; SE p. 689)

Jarrell, "A Girl in a Library" (p. 1166; SE p. 707): Should this poem properly be called an instance of free verse? Or is the underlying pentameter rhythm sufficiently strong that it is rightly called blank verse? What makes this poem feel more like free verse than do Frost's rough pentameters, as in "West-running Brook," for instance (p. 919; SE p. 543)?

Lowell, "The Withdrawal" (p. 1202; SE p. 733)

Bukowski, "Vegas" (p. 1212; SE p. 740): How does the insertion of the kind of poetry that emerges from "poetry class" (lines 11-15) bring attention to the poetic devices Bukowski deliberately avoids in the rest of the poem?

Ammons, "Corsons Inlet" (p. 1255; SE p. 765)

Ginsberg, "In the Baggage Room at Greyhound" (p. 1278; SE p. 776)

Rich, "Transit" (p. 1320; SE p. 803)

Snyder, "Four Poems for Robin" (p. 1330; SE p. 810): The split lines of the first section may allude to the Old English form as imitated in Wilbur's "Junk" (p. 1224; SE p. 747). Why does the last poem fall into groupings of three, four, and five lines? Does this change indicate a growing, retrospective control and ordering, or a sense of loss and fragmentation?

Plath, "Elm" (p. 1351; SE p. 821)

Lorde, "From the House of Yemanjá" (p. 1362; SE p. 829)

Silko, "Prayer to the Pacific" (p. 1402; SE p. 853)

2 STANZAS

A poem written in stanzas comes to a series of temporary endings or completions, if only in the sense that an individual stanza comes to a close. How then does the poem sustain its energy? Sometimes what happens between stanzas can be as important as what happens within them. The list below singles out some notable uses of the stanza, to illustrate the variety of holds—some tight, some slack—that a stanza can have on the design and meaning of a poem. Some poets capitalize on the way stanzas may connect poems written in different eras; Shelley, for instance, borrows and revises established stanza forms such as the Spenserian stanza (in "Adonais") and terza rima (in "Ode to the West Wind"). Other poets, such as Donne, Herbert, Swinburne, and Hardy are particularly inventive in devising new stanza forms for individual poems. In modern and contemporary verse there seems to be a new abundance of virtuosity and energy in inventing stanzas: could this fertility point to a way in which the increased freedom of modern poetry leads to a desire for self-made restrictions?

To describe a stanza fully, you must take into account the number of lines, their length, and the rhyme scheme; for which of the examples on the following list is the treatment of the left-hand margin also a defining feature of the stanza?

Spenser, from *The Faerie Queen*, Book, V, Canto II, stanza 35 (p. 132; SE p. 63): In this stanza Artegall explains God's design of the cosmos: the middle line of the stanza is "The earth was in the middle centre pight"; how does this stanzaic design strengthen Artegall's argument? In which of the other stanzas (which recount an attempt to weigh intangibles in a balance) does the middle (fifth) line serve as a kind of pivot or symmetrical midpoint?

Donne, "Song" ("Go and catch a falling star") (p. 205; SE p. 100) and "The Funeral" (p. 214; SE p. 108)

Herrick, "An Ode for Him" (p. 249; SE p. 131)

Herbert, "Easter Wings" (p. 254; SE p. 133) and "The Flower" (p. 264; SE p. 140)

Swinburne, "The Garden of Proserpine" (p. 839; SE p. 491) and "The Forsaken Garden" (p. 842; SE p. 493)

Hardy, "The Convergence of the Twain" (p. 848; SE p. 499): Do the stanzas "look like" the fatal iceberg? Are they diagrams of the operation of fate (two short, regular lines converge into a longer one)? For what other topics might this curious, bottom-heavy three-line stanza be appropriate? See also Shaped Poems (3.7).

Yeats, "The Stolen Child" (p. 875; SE p. 514), "Byzantium" (p. 890; SE p. 525), and "Long-legged Fly" (p. 893; SE p. 528)

Stevens, "Thirteen Ways of Looking at a Blackbird" (p. 932; SE
    p. 555): For which poems on this list is each stanza a new
    "way of looking" at the poem's subject? Compare the
    function of the three-line stanzas in Steven's "Continual
    Conversation with a Silent Man" (p. 936; SE p. 559).
Eliot, "Preludes" (p. 987; SE p. 597)
Bishop, "Jeronimo's House" (p. 1134; SE p. 691)
Thomas, "The Hunchback in the Park" (p. 1178; SE p. 715)
    and "Fern Hill" (p. 1180; SE p. 717)
Lowell, "This Golden Summer" (p. 1201; SE p. 733): What is
    the effect of each stanza's seeming to take up a somewhat
    different concern, to register a shift in tone and focus?
Dickey, "The Lifeguard" (p. 1231; SE p. 751)
Ammons, "Poetics" (p. 1258; SE p. 765) and "The City
    Limits" (p. 1259; SE p. 769)
Plath, "Black Rook in Rainy Weather" (p. 1345; SE p. 818) and
    "Elm" (p. 1351; SE p. 821): Why did Plath devise a five-line
    stanza for the first of these and a three-line stanza for the
    second? Do there seem to be basic differences (in topic,
    tone, development, etc.) between her poems in five-line
    stanzas ("Black Rook," "The Colossus," "Daddy") and the ones
    in three-lines stanzas ("Elm," "Ariel," "Lady Lazarus")?

2.1 Couplets ("Versification," p. 1413; SE p. 865)

Studying paired lines inevitably touches on a range of important
issues in poetic form. What sorts of differences and affinities may
prevail between the two words that rhyme in a couplet? How do
the rhyming words invite us to look for symmetries, reflections,
imbalances, logical coordinations, etc., between the paired lines as
a whole? How do these questions become especially prominent in
the heroic couplet (see Section 2.2)? Compare the closed couplets
of Augustan satire to the more informal, conversational couplets of
Browning's "My Last Duchess" and to the unrhymed couplets of
Steven's "The House Was Quiet and the World Was Calm." Couplets
in iambic tetrameter— or octosyllabic couplets— are common, from
Milton's "L'Allegro" and "Il Penseroso" to Housman's "Terence,
This is Stupid Stuff ..." and Yeats's "Under Ben Bulben." Varying
effects of linking by rhyme two lines of markedly different length
are illustrated in Herrick's little ode for Ben Johnson (p. 249; SE
p. 131), in the closing couplets of Donne's "The Canonization," and
in Gilbert's "When You're Lying Awake with a Dismal Headache"
(p. 834; SE p. 487). An aphorism by Robert Frost might open up
class discussion: "The couplet is the symbol of the metaphor."

Chaucer, "The Pardoner's Prologue and Tale" (p. 24; SE p. 6)
Anonymous, "The Three Ravens" (p. 73; SE p. 37): What is the
    effect of the refrain's delaying of the second line's completion
    of the first line's sense and rhyme?

Anonymous, "The Silver Swan" (p. 89; SE p. 49)
Nashe, "A Litany in Time of Plague" (p. 202; SE p. 98)
Herrick, "Delight in Disorder" (p. 243; SE p. 126) and "An Ode for Him" (p. 249; SE p. 131)
Marvell, "To His Coy Mistress" (p. 337; SE p. 178)
Milton, "L'Allegro" (p. 284; SE p. 156) and "Il Penseroso" (p. 287; SE p. 159)
Suckling, "Upon My Lady Carlisle's Walking in Hampton Court Garden" (p. 318; SE p. 166)
Pope, "The Rape of the Lock" (p. 409; SE p. 211)
Browning, "My Last Duchess" (p. 717; SE p. 413)
Gilbert, "When You're Lying Awake with a Dismal Headache" (p. 834; SE p. 487)
Housman, "Terence, This Is Stupid Stuff . . ." (p. 865; SE p. 510)
Yeats, "Under Ben Bulben" (p. 895; SE p. 530)
Stevens, "The House Was Quiet and the World Was Calm" (p. 936; SE p. 558)
Jeffers, "Shine, Perishing Republic" (p. 981; SE p. 588)
Owen, "Strange Meeting" (p. 1035; SE p. 624)

2.2 Heroic Couplets ("Versification," p. 1413; SE p. 865)

The closed couplets of eighteenth-century poetry, with their witty antithesis, chiasmic twists of logic, balanced pairings, and droll anticlimaxes, are a good introduction to the rhetoric of poetry as well as to rhyme, lineation, and end-stopping. To get students to focus on the kind of labor that goes into crafting verse of this sort, assign twenty lines or so of any of these poems (say, the section on Belinda's dressing table from "The Rape of the Lock", Canto I, lines 121-40) and ask students to check off how many of these categories each set of rhymes belong in; which rhymes pair different spellings for the same sound (unlocks-box), different parts of speech (arise-eyes), different numbers of syllables (unite-white), different etymologies or even different languages (rows-billet-doux), and—most importantly—different or opposed meanings (arms-charms). They might then make some judgments about which poet pairs rhymes in the most varied and surprising ways.

Wilmot, "A Satire Against Mankind" (p. 385; SE p. 200)
Dryden, "Mac Flecknoe" (p. 369; SE p. 187) and "To the Memory of Mr. Oldham" (p. 374; SE p. 192)
Finch, "A Nocturnal Reverie" (p. 389; SE p. 204)
Swift, "A Description of the Morning" (p. 392; SE p. 206) and "A Description of a City Shower" (p. 392; SE p. 206)
Pope, "The Rape of the Lock" (p. 409; SE p. 211), "Epistle to Miss Blount" (p. 423; SE p. 226)
Montagu, "The Lover: A Ballad" (p. 441; SE p. 237)
Johnson, "The Vanity of Human Wishes" (p. 451; SE p. 238)

2.3 Four-line Stanzas: Quatrains ("Versification," p. 1414; SE p. 866)

Prior, "To a Lady: She Refusing to Continue a Dispute with Me, and Leaving Me in the Argument" (p. 390; SE p. 205)

Gray, "Elegy Written in a Country Churchyard" (p. 463; SE p. 248)

Fitzgerald, "The Rubaiyat of Omar Khayyám of Naishápúr" (p. 684; SE p. 384)

Brontë, "No Coward Soul is Mine" (p. 756; SE p. 436): What is the effect of the alternation of trimeter and pentameter lines? How would the effect be different if the stanza were organized 5-3-5-3 instead of 3-5-3-5? In most quatrains of alternating longer and shorter lines, the shorter lines are lines 2 and 4, not 1 and 3 (for example, popular ballads, Wordsworth, "A Slumber Did My Spirit Seal" [p. 546; SE p. 281]). This exception to the norm invites speculation on why shorter lines tend to follow longer ones and not the other way around.

Pound, "Hugh Selwyn Mauberley" (p. 964; SE p. 576)

Cummings, "somewhere i have never travelled, gladly beyond" (p. 1043; SE p. 630); "anyone lived in a pretty how town" (p. 1044; SE p. 631); "my father moved through dooms of love" (p. 1045; SE p. 632)

Eliot, "Sweeney Among the Nightingales" (p. 999; SE p. 598)

Hope, "Australia" (p. 1108; SE p. 672)

Bishop, "The Armadillo" (p. 1141; SE p. 696)

2.4 Three-line Stanzas: Tercets ("Versification," pp. 1413-14; SE pp. 865-66)

Three-line stanzas are sonewhat rare in poetry in English; certainly they are outnumbered by couplets and quatrains. In which of these poems do tercets have the feeling of a riddle or a somewhat cryptic or incomplete statement? Is it our exposure to quatrains and couplets that tends to make some tercets feel either one line too long or too short?

Herrick, "Upon Julia's Clothes" (p. 248; SE p. 131): To demonstrate the different resources of and responses to tercets, quatrains, and couplets, rewrite this poem in 2- and 4-line units and discuss the effects of these revisions.

Shelley, "Ode to the West Wind" (p. 620; SE p. 337): Does terza rima overcome the potentially incomplete feeling of a three-line stanza by its rhyming linkage (aba bcb cdc, and so on) of each stanza to the next? On terza rima, see "Versification," p. 1414; SE p. 866)

Browning, "A Toccata of Galuppi's" (p. 730; SE p. 426)

Hardy, "The Convergence of the Twain" (p. 848; SE p. 499)

Frost, "Provide, Provide" (p. 921; SE p. 545)

Stevens, "Continual Conversation with a Silent Man" (p. 936; SE p. 559): How do this poem's twangy rhythm and its occasionally folksy language lend to its tercets the shadowy feel of quatrains?

Williams, "Poem" (p. 946; SE p. 562) and "The Yachts" (p. 947; SE p. 562)

Larkin, "Sad Steps" (p. 1231; SE p. 751)

Ammons, "The City Limits" (p. 1259; SE p. 769): How do the three-line stanzas enable one to notice how the repeated phrase "when you consider" shifts about and reappears in different places in the stanza? Rearrange the lines of this poem in the style of Whitman: how does the meaning of natural plenty, energy, "radiance" take on a different meaning? The poem is structured as a long "When . . . then . . ." sentence: how does the stanzaic arrangement help to conceal that structure from the reader, and how does it shape the effect of the discovery, around lines 14-15, that all those "when . . ." clauses are to be answered by a "then . . ." clause?

Walcott, "The Gulf" (p. 1333; SE p. 812)

Plath, "Elm" (p. 1351; SE p. 821). "Ariel" (p. 1353; SE p. 823), "Lady Lazarus" (p. 1354; SE p. 825)

2.5 Other Stanzas ("Versification," pp. 1414-15; SE pp. 866-67)

These seven-, eight-, and nine-line stanzas are relatively rare, and tend to become associated with a few poets or poems. In a more decisive way perhaps even than for the ode or sonnet, for instance, choosing one of these tricky stanzas entails a firm commitment to engage with the literary tradition with which it is linked.

A. Rhyme Royal

Wyatt, "They Flee From Me" (p. 91; SE p. 50)

B. Ottava Rima

Byron, from *Don Juan* (p. 592; SE p. 321)

Yeats, "Sailing to Byzantium" (p. 886; SE p. 522) and "Among School Children" (p. 888; SE p. 524)

C. Spenserian Stanza

Spenser, from *The Faerie Queene* (p. 110; SE p. 62)
Keats, "The Eve of St. Agnes" (p. 650; SE p. 360)
Shelley, "Adonais" (p. 626; SE p. 343)
Tennyson, "The Lotos-Eaters" (p. 700; SE p. 398): The Spenserian
   stanza is used through line 45. What diverse associations has
   the form accumulated by the time Tennyson comes to use it?
   Does Tennyson's model seem to be Spenser himself, or the
   Romantic poets who inherited the Spenserian stanza, or some
   amalgam of the two?

3 FORMS AND GENRES

3.1 Sonnets ("Versification," pp. 1415-17; SE pp. 867-69)

Binding, challenging, and brief, the sonnet form has long been a place for meditations on the very nature of poetic form and its place in the history of poetry. No latter-day poet can write a sonnet without acknowledging in some way—paying homage to, challenging, rethinking—the long line of memorable sonnets that have already been written.

A. Sonnets on the Sonnet

Drayton, from *Idea*, "To the Reader of these Sonnets" (p. 169; SE p. 86)

Wordsworth, "Scorn Not the Sonnet" (p. 561; SE p. 293)

Keats, "On the Sonnet" (p. 657; SE p. 368)

Rossetti, from *The House of Life*, "A Sonnet" (p. 799; SE p. 467)

Meredith, from *Modern Love*, 30 ("What are we first? First, animals; and next") (p. 801; SE p. 469): Sixteen lines long, the poems in *Modern Love* do not fit the sonnet form exactly, of course; but as the last line of this one suggests, they acknowledge in complex ways the tradition of the love sonnet, and the tale of a troubled love, often a love triangle, narrated in such Renaissance sequences as Shakespeare's sonnets.

B. A Sampling of Love Sonnets

Wyatt, "The Long Love That in My Thought Doth Harbor" (p. 89; SE p. 49)

Surrey, "Love, That Doth Reign and Live Within My Thought" (p. 98; SE p. 54)

Spenser, from *Amoretti*, 10 ("Unrighteous Lord of love, what law is this") (p. 135; SE p. 66)

Sidney, from *Astrophel and Stella*, 47 ("What, have I thus betrayed my liberty?") (p. 157; SE p. 81)

Daniel, from *Delia*, 46 ("Let others sing of knights and paladins") (p. 166; SE p. 84)

Drayton, from *Idea*, 6 ("How many paltry, foolish, painted things") (p. 169; SE p. 86)

Shakespeare, Sonnet 138 ("When my love swears that she is made of truth") (p. 190; SE p. 91)

Milton, "Methought I Saw" (p. 294; SE p. 165)

Keats, "When I Have Fears" (p. 649; SE p. 359): Compare to the Elizabethan sonnets that end by praising their own power to

grant immortal fame to a mortal love (such as Spenser's
Sonnet 75, p. 137; SE p. 67; Drayton's Sonnet 6, p. 169; SE
p. 86; and Shakespeare's Sonnets 18, 55, and 65, pp. 186-88;
SE pp. 88-89). Keats's sonnet ends when "Love and Fame to
nothingness do sink." On what basis then can this be considered a love sonnet?

E. B. Browning, "Sonnets from the Portuguese," 43 ("How do I love
thee? Let me count the ways") (p. 674; SE p. 380)

D. G. Rossetti, "Silent Noon" (p. 799; SE p. 468)

Millay, "I, Being Born a Woman and Distressed" (p. 1033; SE
p. 624)

Berryman, Sonnet 23 ("They may suppose, because I would not cloy
your ear") (p. 1162; SE p. 704)

Heaney, from *Glanmore Sonnets*, 10 ("I dreamt we slept in a moss
in Donegal") (p. 1385; SE p. 843)

C. Devotional or Religious Sonnets

Donne, from *Holy Sonnets*, 14 ("Batter my heart, three-personed
God") (p. 222; SE p. 113)

Herbert, "Sin (I)" (p. 254; SE p. 134) and "Prayer (I)" (p. 256; SE
p. 135)

Milton, "When I Consider How My Light Is Spent" and "On the
Late Massacre in Piedmont" (p. 293; SE p. 164)

Hopkins, "[Thou Art Indeed Just, Lord . . .]" (p. 860; SE p. 506)

D. Other Sonnets

How does the range of topics treated in sonnet form expand after
the Elizabethan period?

Milton, "Cyriack, Whose Grandsire" (p. 293; SE p. 164)

Wordsworth, "It Is a Beauteous Evening" (p. 549; SE p. 284)

Shelley, "England in 1819" (p. 620; SE p. 337): Compare
Wordsworth's sonnet, "London, 1802" (p. 550; SE p. 285).

Keats, "On First Looking into Chapman's Homer" (p. 648; SE
p. 359)

Poe, "Sonnet—To Science" (p. 694; SE p. 393)

Arnold, "Shakespeare" (p. 782; SE p. 457)

Meredith, "Lucifer in Starlight" (p. 803; SE p. 471)

C. Rossetti, "In an Artist's Studio" (p. 818; SE p. 479)

Hopkins, "[No Worst, There Is None. Pitched Past Pitch of Grief]"
(p. 858; SE p. 505)

Yeats, "Leda and the Swan" (p. 888; SE p. 523)

Frost, "The Oven Bird" (p. 914; SE p. 541) and "Design" (p. 921;
SE p. 545)

Ransom, "Piazza Piece" (p. 1019; SE 616)

MacDiarmid, "In the Children's Hospital" (p. 1027; SE p. 620)

Millay, "Euclid Alone Has Looked on Beauty Bare" (p. 1033; SE
     p. 623)
Owen, "Anthem for Doomed Youth" (p. 1036; SE p. 625)
Cummings, "the Cambridge ladies who live in furnished souls"
     (p. 1041; SE p. 628)
Crane, "To Emily Dickinson" (p. 1061; SE p. 644)
Kavanagh, "Inniskeen Road: July Evening" (p. 1087; SE p. 659)
Hayden, "Those Winter Sundays" (p. 1158; SE p. 701)
Lowell, "1930's" and "Harriet" (p. 1201; SE p. 732)
Hill, from "Apology for the Revival of Christian Architecture in
     England" (9 "The Laurel Axe") (p. 1344; SE p. 818)

3.2 Sonnet Sequences

This anthology prints no sonnet sequences entire: in what ways
does the anthology misrepresent these sonnets by isolating them?
A question for class discussion: does this anthology misrepresent
the sonnets more than it does the other poems it necessarily
isolates from the volume or canon from which they were selected?

Spenser, "Amoretti" (p. 135; SE p. 66)
Sidney, *Astrophel and Stella* (p. 156; SE p. 80)
Daniel, "Delia" (p. 165; SE p. 83)
Drayton, "Idea" (p. 169; SE p. 86)
Shakespeare, Sonnets (p. 186; SE p. 88)
Donne, Holy Sonnets (p. 220; SE p. 112)
Meredith, *Modern Love* (p. 801; SE p. 469)

3.3 Other Sequences

Long poems that are groups of shorter poems, which may be of the
same or different lengths and forms, can be represented in the
anthology only by selections; the same questions might be asked of
the poems listed below as of the sonnets excerpted from Sonnet
Sequences (3.2). Why in the modern period have lyric sequences
replaced epic as the mode of the long poem? What permutations
in tone, attitude, language, etc. are undergone by the speaking
voice in these selections? How are these different when the
sequence is comprised of identical stanza forms (Tennyson, Hill)
and when it is composed of sections of varying form and length
(Whitman, Pound)? The selection from "In Memoriam" perhaps
gives the best feel of the challenges and dynamics of lyric
sequences.

Tennyson, "In Memoriam A. H. H." (p. 706; SE p. 405)
Whitman, "Song of Myself" (p. 760; SE p. 438)
Pound, "High Selwyn Mauberley: Life and Contacts" (p. 964; SE
     p. 576)

Berryman, "The Dream Songs" (p. 1162; SE p. 705)
Hill, "Mercian Hymns" (p. 1341; SE p. 816)

3.4 Ballad

How do ballads narrate events? Why do ballads often begin at the climax, or even aftermath, of their stories? Compare the modern ballads of Housman, Betjeman, and Auden with the anonymous folk or popular ballads (pp. 68-84; SE pp. 34-46). In what ways do these literary ballads—written to be read, not sung—allude to the conventions of popular ballads? In what ways do they suggest that the world has changed so radically since the days of "Lord Randall" and his kin, that the values of folk ballads are no longer tenable? (This conjunction of old and new could also be taught under the topic of allusion; see Section 8.1.)

Coleridge, "The Rime of the Ancient Mariner" (p. 567; SE p. 298)
Dickinson, Poem 712 ("Because I could not stop for Death—")
  (p. 812; SE p. 476): In its riddling way of telling a story of a
  ghoulish courtship, how is this poem somewhat reminiscent of
  popular ballads like "The Unquiet Grave" (p.75; SE p. 39)?
Housman, "Is my Team Plowing" (p. 863; SE p. 508)
Betjeman, "The Arrest of Oscar Wilde at the Cadogan Hotel"
  (p. 1095; SE p. 665)
Auden, "As I Walked Out One Evening" (p. 1099; SE p. 667)

3.5 Villanelle ("Versification," pp. 1417-18; SE pp. 869-70)

The villanelle could be taught in conjunction with couplets, as the pattern of the villanelle might be thought of as an intricate delaying of the coming together of the first and third lines as a couplet closing the poem: what transformations and groupings must these two lines each undergo or participate in separately before they can act as a couplet? How does this delay reinforce the villanelle's sense of finality?

Roethke, "The Waking" (p. 1119; SE p. 680): How is the poem
  different if you put a comma in line 3 after "going," or after
  "learn"? That is, at what point in this poem are we likely to
  decide that the richly ambiguous third line means "I learn
  wherever it is I have to go, simply by the act of going there,"
  and not "I learn (whatever it is I learn) by going where I know
  I must go?" Or does the line hover somewhere between those
  two meanings? If so, how does the pattern of the villanelle
  help to keep both senses of the line in play?

Thomas, "Do Not Go Gentle into That Good Night" (p. 1181; SE p. 718): Although the crucial first and third lines of Thomas's villanelle do not share the shimmering ambiguities of Roethke's lines, how do they undergo changes of meaning as they recur? Where do the lines' imperatives become indicative verbs, and what is the effect of this shift?

3.6 Sestina ("Versification," p. 1418; SE p. 870)

Although an eccentric, difficult, and rare form, the sestina is useful for teaching the way poets can alter and refine the meaning of a word through repeating it in different contexts throughout a poem. The changing contexts of the end-words of a sestina make the words accumulate a series of associations much as rhyme often does—that is, the changing partners a word accumulates in a rhyme scheme create a halo of associations for that word. A successful sestina is such a display of virtuosity that it reminds us that "poetry" is literally "making," and that a poem can be an intricately crafted artifact, a made thing, as well as an expressive utterance, a heartfelt response. Jon Stallworthy suggests that in writing such complicated forms as the sestina and the villanelle, poets aim for "the graceful momentum of good dancing" ("Versification," p. 1418; SE p. 870); you might ask students to compare these two ways of thinking about elaborately patterned poems: are such poems more like crafted artifacts or like intricate dances?

The sestina is so rigid and yet flexible a pattern that it can be a useful form to experiment with as a class exercise: invent a title, choose six words, arrange them in the order in which they must appear at the ends of the lines in six stanzas, and have groups of students collaborate to write a stanza each. To give students a good idea of the kind of exercise Hecht set himself, in the instance below, make the six words as varied in sound and reference as possible, but choose some words that may also be used as different parts of speech; to make a more Sidneyan sestina, choose six common monosyllabic words of Anglo-Saxon derivation.

Sidney, "Ye Goatherd Gods" (p. 153; SE p. 77): A double sestina.
Bishop, "Sestina" (p. 1142; SE p. 697): How do the six recurring words of the sestina figure the repetitive, enclosed household of child and grandmother?
Hecht, "Sestina d'Inverno" (p. 1237; SE p. 755): How does the sestina form suit life in Rochester as Hecht pictures it? How does the end-word "Rochester" make the pattern of the sestina more visible?
Ashbery, "The Painter" (p. 1288; SE p. 784)

3.7 Shaped Poems ("Versification," p. 1422; SE p. 874)

As with onomatopoeia (see Sounds, Section 5.2), which does not make words sound like non-verbal sounds except largely by conventional association between the sound of the word and what the word means, one should be cautious about claiming that the shapes on the page of these oddly formed poems actually picture the objects they describe. Herbert's poem looks like wings (and not, say, an hourglass or a dish for an ice cream sundae) because the title suggests the resemblance, and because the poem looks like other poems so shaped and titled. All poems are poem-shaped; some poems are shaped like other shaped poems, and only by that association can they be said to look like or be shaped like the things they are about. How do shaped poems explicate the meaning of the things they are shaped like, combining picture and explanatory caption in a shaped text?

Assigning students to write their own shaped poems (with the advent of the word processor, the possibilities seem endless) is a good way to sharpen their sense of the physical format of poems generally, and to show how necessity can be the mother of invention when a certain idea must be fit into a prepatterned grid.

Herbert, "Easter Wings" (p. 254; SE p. 133): An exercise: have
    students, using a typewriter, write a variation on this poem,
    called "Easter Eggs": what different views of Easter may
    emerge from a poem whose shape bulges rather than thins in
    the middle?
Hardy, "The Convergence of the Twain" (p. 848; SE p. 499): Jon
    Stallworthy notes, in the "Versification" essay, that "the shape
    of the stanza suggests the iceberg that is the poem's subject"
    (p. 1407; SE p. 859). Might it suggest the ship as well?
Cummings, "r-p-o-p-h-e-s-s-a-g-r" (p. 1044; SE p. 631) and "1(a"
    (p. 1047; SE p. 634): Cummings's game is clearly different
    from Herbert's and Hollander's; rather than a block of set type
    "in the shape of" the poem's subject, these poems depend for
    their effect on exploding the usual blocky shape of a printed
    poem. We can read the Herbert and Hollander poems aloud
    with no difficulty, but try assigning your students to read these
    two Cummings poems aloud. In "1(a" the double joke about
    loneliness as "one-liness" becomes clearer if you type the
    poem out on a typewriter that uses the same key for the Arabic
    numeral *one* and the lower case *L*, as of course Cummings did.
Hollander, "Swan and Shadow" (p. 1308; SE p. 796): The poem is
    about a sight that is transient, hard to see, hard to make out;
    the poem itself—by virtue of its being a shaped poem—is
    permanent, an obvious picture, instantly declaring its subject:
    is there a way to resolve this contradiction?

3.8 Song

What makes some poems more suitable than others to be set to music or sung? Listed here, among other songs, are most of the poems that are titled "Song"; but this label clearly means different things in different instances. So many poets with highly varied designs and ambitions have called their works "songs"—from *Songs of Innocence and Experience* to "Song of Myself" to "The Love Song of J. Alfred Prufrock" to "The Dream Songs—that we may wonder what power and resonance such a label is thought to hold. Which features of traditional song—Renaissance love lyrics, or Dryden's "A Song for St. Cecilia's Day," or lyrics commissioned for a musical setting—do Whitman and Eliot and Ashbery wish to invoke when they call their poems "songs"? See also Section 7.20, Music.

Anonymous, "Jolly Good Ale and Old" (p. 61; SE p. 30): Compare this drinking song to Lyly's "Oh, For a Bowl of Fat Canary" (p. 152; SE p. 76).

Anonymous, "Fine Knacks for Ladies" (p. 87; SE p. 47)

Shakespeare, "It Was a Lover and His Lass" (p. 194; SE p. 92) is marked for singing by its recurrent nonsense refrain, mere place-fillers that serve to carry the tune and enable listeners to join in whether they know the words to the song or not. "Oh Mistress Mine" (p. 195; SE p. 93) and "When That I Was a Little Tiny Boy" (p. 195; SE p. 93) might be taught as a unit, since they both come from *Twelfth Night.*

Campion, "My Sweetest Lesbia" (p. 198; SE p. 95), and all the other Campion selections, were written to be sung to lute accompaniment: what features do they share that make them singable? In which poems does Campion seem to have been hard pressed to make sure that all the stanzas of a song will fit equally well into the same tune? In "When to Her Lute Corinna Sings" (p. 199; SE p. 95), what is the relation between voice and instrument? Compare Corinna as a singer with Campion's "Rose-cheeked Laura" (p. 200; SE p. 96), and her "beauty's / silent music." Compare also Marvell's "The Fair Singer" (p. 340; SE p. 181).

Donne, "Song" ("Go and catch a falling star") (p. 205; SE p. 100) and "Song" ("Sweetest love, I do not go") (p. 208; SE p. 103): What makes these better texts for singing than other poems by Donne in the anthology?

Jonson, "Song: To Celia" (p. 230; SE p. 120) and "Come, My Celia" (p. 237; SE p. 121)

Waller, "Song" ("Go, lovely rose!") (p. 274; SE p. 146)

Suckling, "Song" ("Why so pale and wan, fond lover") (p. 317; SE p. 166)

Dryden, "A Song for St. Cecilia's Day" (p. 375; SE p. 193)

Blake, "Song" ("How sweet I roam'd from field to field") (p. 496; SE p. 258)

Byron, "So We'll Go No More A-Roving" (p. 592; SE p. 321): This poem has been set to music; see under Rhyme, Section 1.4.

Lear, "The Owl and the Pussy-Cat" (p. 750; SE p. 433): This poem has been set to music.

Christina Rossetti, "Song" ("When I am dead, my dearest") (p. 817; SE p. 479)

Gilbert, "Titwillow" (p. 836; SE p. 489): What marks this poem as something of a parody of Renaissance songs? Which features of the Renaissance selections on this list does it spoof or exaggerate? The challenge they present to the singer is part of the humor of Gilbert's patter songs, which are usually delivered at a breathtaking clip, half-sung, half-recited; examples are "When You're Lying Awake with a Dismal Headache" (p. 834; SE p. 487) and "I Am the Very Model of a Modern Major-General" (p. 833; SE p. 486).

Tennyson, Song from *The Princess* (p. 705; SE p. 403)

Eliot, "The Love Song of J. Alfred Prufrock" (p. 994; SE p. 594)

Bogan, "Song for the Last Act" (p. 1053; SE p. 638)

Ammons, "Small Song" (p. 1258; SE p. 768)

Gunn, "Street Song" (p. 1305; SE p. 794): Compare to the anonymous song, "Fine Knacks for Ladies" (p. 87; SE p. 47), also sung by a street vendor to peddle his wares.

Atwood, "Pig Song" (p. 1376; SE p. 837)

3.9 Hymn

Poets have labeled their poems "hymns" with the same diversity of intent as they call their poems "songs." I have included here all the poems explicitly titled "hymns," but as with the listing under Song, the differences will tend to be more instructive than the similarities. As hymns are generally poems of address to God or a god, they may be taught along with questions of address or apostrophe (Section 5.7). The poems by Watts, Cowper, and Dickinson may be usefully taught as a group in conjunction with song. What restrictions do Cowper and Watts labor under in composing religious poems designed to be sung by a congregation to a simple tune? Compare Cowper's and Watts's hymns for music to the more personal entreaties of Donne, Jonson, Crashaw, and Dickinson. On hymn meters, see ""Versification," p. 1414; SE p. 866.

Donne, "Hymn to God My God, in My Sickness" (p. 223; SE p. 113)

Jonson, "A Hymn to God the Father" (p. 231; SE p. 120): How does the two-beat meter reflect the speaker's "broken heart"?

Watts, "Our God, Our Help" (p. 400; SE p. 209): What features of this hymn (in common meter) would make it easy for a congregation to sing it in unison?

Cowper, "Olney Hymns" (p. 480; SE p. 255): Is Cowper's or Watts's hymn easier to sing? How do both Cowper and Watts give the congregation time to catch their breath while singing? Which hymn is easier for the worshippers to understand while they are singing it?

Crashaw, "A Hymn to the Name and Honor of the Admirable Saint Teresa" (p. 327; SE p. 172)

Dickinson, Poem 258 ("There's a certain Slant of light") (p. 806; SE p. 474) and Poem 1129 ("Tell all the Truth but tell it slant—"(p. 815; SE p. 478): Compared to Cowper and Watts, the heterodox, "slant" nature of Dickinson's private hymns (or the degree to which this label is accurate) become easier to see. Why can we imagine a congregation singing Watts's hymn, but not Dickinson's poems, although these are written almost entirely in some form of hymn meters? (Yet Aaron Copland has set some of Dickinson's poems to music.)

Shelley, "Hymn to Intellectual Beauty" (p. 614; SE p. 334): What conventions of address and entreaty does Shelley borrow from religious hymns?

Emerson, "Concord Hymn" (p. 665; SE p. 375)

Atwood, "Pig Song" (p. 1376; SE p. 838): The last line is "This is a hymn"; a hymn to what?

3.10 Epic ("Versification," p. 1403; SE p. 855)

An introductory course in lyric poetry will rarely have time to study an epic in its entirety; yet selections from epic can suggest the form's scope and ambitions, and its relation to lyric and other, briefer poetic forms. If classical epics typically narrate the voyages of empire-foundtic or heroes, Romantic epics transform such national journeys into personal, internal ones (Wordsworth's *Prelude*). Should an epic in this century be national (or global?) or autobiographical? A question for class discussion: why hasn't there been an epic poem on the voyage to the moon? or on the risk of nuclear holocaust? (Is it just that our sensibility cannot accommodate the conventions of epic any longer? Or have movies or other forms of culture or entertainment taken over some of the functions and ambitions of epic poetry? What answer to these questions does Creeley's "Heroes" suggest?) An exercise: write the opening lines—including invocation to the muse (*which* muse is part of the problem)—to a modern epic on the moon landings or on nuclear war. Will the result necessarily be mock epic? See also the section on Mythology, 8.3.

Spenser, from *The Faerie Queene*, Book V, Canto II, stanzas 29-50 (p. 131; SE p. 62)

Milton, from *Paradise Lost*, Book I [The Invocation] (p. 295; SE p. 165)

Wordsworth, from *The Prelude*, Book I, lines 301-475 ("Fair seedtime had my soul, and I grew up") (p. 538; SE p. 276)

Whitman, from "Song of Myself": Is Whitman's long personal poem an epic? Section 1 ("I celebrate myself and sing myself") (p. 760; SE p. 438) and Section 24 ("Walt Whitman, a kosmos, of Manhattan the son") (p. 762; SE p. 440) are most pertinent to this issue.

Pound, from *The Cantos*, Canto I ("And then went down to the ship") (p. 976; SE p. 583)

Creeley, "Heroes" (p. 1271; SE p. 776)

3.11 Mock Epic

It may be easier to teach the conventions of epic poetry through their parodies than through epics themselves. Among other issues, Pope's story of Belinda should raise the question of why the heroes of epic poems are invariably men, and whether an epic poem could be written about a woman.

Pope, "The Rape of the Lock" (p. 409; SE p. 211)

Byron, from Don Juan, Canto the First, stanzas 1-117 (p. 592; SE p. 321)

3.12 Narrative

Students may tend to think of poems as moments of emotion or contemplation, but it is important to remind them that poems can also tell stories. Perhaps all poems do, even very short ones; what kind of story might we invent as background for "Western Wind," for example? Or maybe it is more accurate to say that all poems have a plot, or at least follow some progression or narrative of their own unfolding (see Section 4.3, on Middles). Most of the Popular Ballads (pp. 68-84; SE pp. 34-46) tell stories, often in highly abbreviated ways; I've listed only a few here that seem especially useful for helping students reflect on how poems do so. Story poems can be long, detailed yarns ("The Rime of the Ancient Mariner") or blunt, tight-lipped recountings of a life ("The Death of the Ball Turret Gunner"). So many poems could be said to give an account of events or unfold a tale of some kind that this list can attempt merely to suggest the range possible in narrative poems.

Anonymous, "Jolly Jankin" (p. 57; SE p. 27)

Anonymous, "Sir Patrick Spens" (p. 74; SE p. 38) and "Mary Hamilton" (p. 80; SE p. 42)

Herbert, "The Pulley" (p. 263; SE p. 139): This poem is like a "just-so story," telling how something came about, giving the story that resulted in a present condition—in this case, why human beings are always restless and unsatisfied, no matter what blessings they enjoy.

Blake, "I Asked a Thief" (p. 507; SE p. 265)

Coleridge, "The Rime of the Ancient Mariner" (p. 567; SE p. 298)

Keats, "The Eve of St. Agnes" (p. 650; SE p. 360)

Poe, "Annabel Lee" (p. 697; SE p. 395)

Browning, "My Last Duchess" (p. 717; SE 413)

Arnold, "The Scholar-Gypsy" (p. 783; SE p. 458): You might treat this poem as a ghost story.

Dickinson, Poem 712 ("Because I could not stop the Death—") (p. 812; SE p. 476)

Housman, "Is My Team Plowing" (p. 863; SE p. 508)

Yeats, "Lapis Lazuli" (p. 891; SE p. 527): What kind of a story does the speaker find in or fabricate about the carved figures? Compare to the kinds of little narratives told about the scenes on the urn in Keats's "Ode on a Grecian Urn" (p. 663; SE p. 372)

Robinson, "Eros Turannos" (p. 901; SE p. 534): Why is this poem skeptical about the ability of a narrative account to tell the full truth about a relationship between two people ("as if the story of a house were told, or ever could be")?

De la Mare, "The Listeners" (p. 906; SE p. 538)

Frost, "The Road Not Taken" (p. 913; SE p. 540): This is perhaps a good introductory poem for this group, as it invites discussion of the ways we tell stories about our lives in order to make sense of them. If the two roads were about the same, how could it have made all the difference which one the speaker chose? Why is it more comforting to think of our lives as irrevocably shaped by proceeding through a series of crucial forks in the road, than as simply one long continuous journey of random routes? Compare with the picture Coleridge's Ancient Mariner gives of the decisions or accidents that shaped the journey of his life.

Jarrell, "The Death of the Ball Turret Gunner" (p. 1166; SE p. 707): How does Jarrell tell a whole life in five lines? What sort of a life is it that can be told so tersely? Exercise: rewrite "The Rime of the Ancient Mariner," or any of the poems in this list, in five lines or so, using Jarrell's poem as a model.

O'Hara, "The Day Lady Died" (p. 1285; SE p. 781)

3.13 Dramatic Monologue

This is a specialized genre, central to the topics listed under Section 5, Language, Voice, and Address. The designation "dramatic monologue" can be a bit misleading, as the speaker of these poems does not, as a rule, soliloquize on a bare stage. The speaker of a dramatic monologue generally has a listener. In which poems does the speaker's continuing to talk seem to depend most heavily on the listener's lending an ear?

Wordsworth, "Lines Composed a Few Miles Above Tintern Abbey" (p. 523; SE p. 273): This poem is not generally labeled a dramatic monologue, but in the context of the Tennyson and Browning selections, the discovery around line 114 that the speaker's sister accompanies him can begin to change our sense of the speaker's meditative isolation.

Tennyson, "Ulysses" (p. 704; SE p. 402) and "Tithonus" (p. 713; SE p. 411)

Browning, "My Last Duchess" (p. 717; SE p. 413), "The Bishop Orders His Tomb at Saint Praxed's Church" (p. 720; SE p. 416), "Fra Lippo Lippi" (p. 723; SE p. 419), and "Andrea del Sarto" (p. 737; SE p. 428)

3.14 Ode   ("Versification," p. 1419; SE p. 871)

Roethke puns bawdily on the terms designating the parts of an ode in "I Knew a Woman": "She taught me Turn, and Counter-turn, and Stand" (p. 1120; SE p. 680, line 9). What is the point of alluding to lovemaking in terms of an ode?

Gray, "Ode: On the Death of a Favorite Cat, Drowned in a Tub of Goldfishes" (p. 462; SE p. 247): What features of the genre does this mock ode poke fun at?

Collins, "Ode on the Poetical Character" (p. 467; SE p. 251)

Wordsworth, "Ode: Intimations of Immortality" (p. 551; SE p. 286)

Coleridge, "Dejection: An Ode" (p. 581; SE p. 312)

Shelley, "Ode to the West Wind" (p. 620; SE p. 337). Is "To a Skylark" an ode? Compare how Shelley addresses these two subjects.

Keats, "Ode to a Nightingale" (p. 660; SE p. 370); "Ode on Melancholy" (p. 662; SE p. 371); "Ode on a Grecian Urn" (p. 663; SE 372)

3.15 Elegy

Poems commemorating a death introduce considerations of how a poem's occasion is related to its structure. How does the loss that prompts the writing of elegies shape a poet's decisions about how to structure the poem and how to follow, reshape, or depart from inherited conventions of writing such poems? How do poems of mourning tend to begin and end? How do poets work toward some consolation that enables them to bring their laments to a satisfying close? What kinds of special demands on language are made by the poet's need to come to terms with death, and experience the poet cannot know directly? How do poems on the death of children differ from poems on the death of spouses, friends, poets, or heads of state? What resources do poets invent to find solace for the loss of a child? of a fellow poet?

Poems can be arranged according to the degree and kind of consolation they achieve. Which poets seem inconsolable? How do the ways elegies end, and the kinds of solace they find, shift from earlier, Christian poems to later ones, in which the comforts of faith in an afterlife— or in the reassurances of the elegiac conventions themselves— may no longer be available? For a recent historical survey of the elegy, that addresses these questions through detailed readings of the major examples, see Peter M. Sacks, *The English Elegy: Studies in the Genre from Spenser to Yeats* (Baltimore: Johns Hopkins University Press, 1985).

The anthology includes a great many elegies; I have compiled first a random introductory list, followed by groupings according to the person or persons the elegy commemorates. For poems on the deaths of soldiers, see the section on War (7.5).

A. A Gathering of Elegies

D'Orléans, "Oft in My Thought"(p. 53; SE p. 22): How has the poet continued to keep his thoughts busy with the task of finding the best gift for his beloved? What constraints does the refrain put on the elegizing poet?

Tichborne, "Tichborne's Elegy" (p. 105; SE p. 58): How do the elegance and restraint of Tichborne's figures for his paradoxical condition save the poem from any tinge of maudlin self-pity?

Hayman, "Of the Great and Famous Ever-to-be-honored Knight, Sir Francis Drake, and of My Little-Little Self" (p. 203; SE p. 99): What is the effect of the first mention of Drake's name at the end of a string of adjectives? How does the anecdote of a childhood brush with greatness suggest that the poet laments his own inadequacies as much as he laments Drake's death?

Shakespeare, "Fear No More the Heat o' the Sun" (p. 196; SE p. 94): Does the gentle pun at the end of the refrain seem in poor taste for a dirge? Compare to the puns in Jonson's "On My First Son" (p. 224; SE p. 115).

Browne, "On the Countess Dowager of Pembroke" (p. 241; SE p. 125): How does Browne give the reader the last responsibility for commemorating the Countess?

Herrick, "Upon Prue, His Maid" (p. 249; SE p. 131)

Johnson, "On the Death of Dr. Robert Levet" (p. 458; SE p. 246)

Landor, "Rose Aylmer" (p. 585; SE p. 316)

Poe, "Annabel Lee" (p. 697; SE p. 395)

Tennyson, from "*In Memoriam A. H. H.*" (p. 706; SE p. 405):
Compare the endings of sections 7, 50, and 95. How are
memories of Hallam linked to particular places and times of
day?

Brontë, "Remembrance" (p. 754; SE p. 435)

Whitman, "When Lilacs Last in the Dooryard Bloom'd" (p. 775; SE
p. 450): How does Whitman combine a sense of personal and
national mourning? Compare the voice of the bird in section
14 with other imagined voices in elegies, as in Wordsworth's
"Three Years She Grew" and Milton's "Lycidas."

Hardy, "Thoughts of Phena" (p. 844; SE p.495)

Baxter, "Lament for Barney Flanagan" (p. 1264; SE p. 772): Pair
with Ginsberg, "Aunt Rose," as examples of elegies for people
given rather unflattering portraits.

Tate, "The Lost Pilot" (p. 1391; SE p. 846): How do the surviving
gunner and co-pilot help to reconcile the son to his father's
death? Compare this one to other elegies that argue that an
early death is better than survival into decay and age (such as
Dryden, "To the Memory of Mr. Oldham, p. 374; SE p. 192,
and most of the elegies for children listed below). How does
the son, as a survivor, compare himself with the gunner and
co-pilot?

B. Elegies for Children

Jonson, "On My First Daughter" (p. 224; SE p. 114) and"On My
First Son" (p. 224; SE p. 115): How do Jonson's strategies of
consolation differ for a male and female child? See Bradstreet,
"The Author to Her Book" (p. 324: SE p. 169) for another
comparison of a child to a poem. "Epitaph on Salomon Pavy, a
Child of Queen Elizabeth's Chapel" (p. 228; SE p. 117): How
does Jonson make his "little story" about the boy actor's death
into a poem of praise for his artistry? How do meter and
rhyme scheme mark a difference in tone between "Salomon
Pavy" and the elegies for Jonson's own children?

Herrick, "Upon Wedlock, and Death of Children" (p. 383; SE
p. 198): How does the elaborate conceit of the children as
flowers help the poet find consolation? What is the effect of
the repeated act of concession? (Compare the fifth and
seventh stanzas.) Would the poem be more convincing if it
ended at line 30?

Wordsworth, "Three Years She Grew" (p. 545; SE p. 280): What
prompts the invention of the voice of Nature? Compare the
solace Wordsworth finds in the child's return to Nature and
that Taylor finds in his children's return to the Lord. Compare
the child-flower metaphor in each.

Housman, "To an Athlete Dying Young" (p. 862; SE p. 507): Its
ascribing to the dead a Hellenic, heroic end makes this poem a
good contrast to elegies with a more Christian consolation.

Ransom, "Bells for John Whiteside's Daughter" (p. 1018; SE p. 616): What is the function of the vignette in stanzas 2-4 of the girl chasing the geese? Compare this passage to Nature's description of the girl in Wordsworth, "Three Years She Grew."

Roethke, "Elegy for Jane" (p. 1118; SE p. 679): Compare to Wordsworth's and Ransom's elegies for girls: why does Roethke see Jane as a bird? Why is consolation so difficult for him to find?

Thomas, "A Refusal to Mourn the Death, by Fire, of a Child in London" (p. 1179; SE p. 716): In what sense is Thomas's refusal a rebuttal to other poems on this list? Why does he see elegy as a kind of blasphemy?

Ammons, "Easter Morning" (p. 1261; SE p. 769): Does the closing vision of the two birds afford the poet any consolation? Compare with other Easter poems: despite its title, does this poem actually call on the assurances of the Christian idea of resurrection? Or compare with other poems marking a return to a place (Wordsworth, "Tintern Abbey") or a return to a childhood home (Hugo, "White Center"). What features does "Easter Morning," which recalls a child's death many years before the poet's act of remembrance, share with poems written soon after the child's death?

Stallworthy, "The Almond Tree" (p. 1366; SE p. 831): The allusion to Jonson's "On My First Son" in stanza 4 invites a comparison of the two elegies: in what sense may Stallworthy's narrative of a son's birth be considered an elegy? Compare the almond tree to other figures of natural growth in this group of poems.

Heaney, "Mid-term Break" (p. 1379; SE p. 839)

C. Elegies for Brothers

This group illustrates how varied can be the poems prompted by the same loss— the death of a brother. How do poems on the loss of a member of the poet's own generation differ from those on the deaths of members of an older or younger generation?

Wordsworth, "Elegiac Stanzas" (p. 558; SE p. 290): Like Tennyson's "Frater Ave Atque Vale," this poem seems occasioned as much by another work of art as by a death. How does the death of his brother enable the poet to approve Beaumont's stormy picture of a sight the poet has witnessed as serene?

Tennyson, "Frater Ave Atque Vale" (p. 716; SE p. 412): How has Tennyson linked two acts of remembrance: of his brother, and of Catullus' poem? Compare to other poems in which remembrance of the deceased is linked to a particular landscape, such as Ammons's "Easter Morning."

Muir, "The Brothers" (p. 993; SE p. 593): More a reminiscence, perhaps, than an elegy, though you might ask the class to refine this distinction. Compare to other poems on dreams. Ammons, "Easter Morning" (p. 1261; SE p. 769)

D. Elegies for Poets

Dunbar, "Lament for the Makaris" (p. 62; SE p. 30): Not all elegies for poets insist that their verse makes them immortal. In Dunbar's list of the poets whom death has mown down, why is there so little sense that their lines prolong their lives?

Surrey, "Wyatt Resteth Here" (p. 98; SE p. 55): As in Jonson's elegy for Shakespeare, elegies for poets often undertake rankings of poetic greatness. What role did poetic rivalry play in Wyatt's art? Compare the nationalistic strain in a number of these Renaissance elegies: the insistence that these poets bring glory to Britain reminds us that writers of verse in English often felt themselves inferior to classical and Continental poets.

Jonson, "To the Memory of My Beloved, the Author Mr. William Shakespeare" (p. 239; SE p. 123): What is the effect of the hesitancies and false starts of lines 1-17? How would our sense of the relation between Shakespeare and Jonson be different if the poem began with "Soul of the Age!" Why does Jonson insist that Shakespeare's greatness is as much "Art" as "Nature"? Along with this poem assign some of Shakespeare's songs and sonnets, and ask the class to consider what features of them Jonson might have admired, on the basis of his elegy. Compare Jonson's praise with what Shakespeare says of his own poetry's immortality (Sonnets 55, 65).

Herrick, "Upon Ben Jonson" (p. 249; SE p. 131): How is this little poem an argument against the elegiac mode? "An Ode for Him" (p. 249; SE 131): What is the effect of the increasing line lengths in each stanza?

Carew, "An Elegy upon the Death of the Dean of Paul's, Dr. John Donne" (p. 272; SE p. 144): Assign some of Donne's poems and ask the class to find examples of the kinds of purgation and weeding out of poetic language that Carew ascribes to Donne. What Donne-like touches in Carew's elegy attest to the truth of his claims about Donne's verse? How does Carew handle the tricky assignment of paying tribute to a poet who began writing secular, often erotic, poetry, but who ended his career as a priest and religious poet?

Milton, "Lycidas" (p. 275; SE p. 147): How are the strategies of consolation different for the death of a young poet (here, Edward King; Dryden's elegy for Oldham; Shelley's for Keats) and the death of an older one who has fulfilled his promise (Surrey on Wyatt, Jonson on Shakespeare, Carew on Donne)?

How does Milton make use of the special circumstances of King's death by drowning? Consider the progression of kinds of "false surmise" (line 153) and compare them to those in other poems in this group.

Dryden, "To the Memory of Mr. Oldham" (p. 374; SE p. 192): What is the effect of the alexandrines (six-beat lines or hexameters) at lines 21 and 25? At the beginning of the poem, Oldham and Dryden seem to be almost twins: how does the distance between them increase as the poem progresses?

Wordsworth, "Extempore Effusion upon the Death of James Hogg" (p. 561; SE p. 294): How does an elegy in quatrains arrive at consolation differently from stichic ones—that is, ones not broken into stanzas? Like Dunbar, Wordsworth lists his fellow poets whom death has taken: compare Dunbar and Wordsworth as "frail survivors" (line 36). How does Wordsworth link the poets he names with particular landscapes or places? Compare line 35 with lines 19-21 in "Oldham."

Coleridge, "Epitaph" (p. 585; SE p. 315): Why does Coleridge's epitaph for himself ask for forgiveness rather than fame? Compare to Yeats's epitaph for himself in "Under Ben Bulben" (p. 895; SE p. 530).

Shelley, "Adonais" (p. 626; SE p. 353): This compendium of elegiac devices is perhaps best taught toward the end of a unit on the elegy. Does Shelley give us a sense of what Keats was like as a poet, in the way Carew does for Donne? Compare with other poems on the early death of a poet ("Lycidas," "To the Memory of Mr. Oldham").

Berryman, Dream Song 324, "An Elegy for W. C. W., The Lovely Man" (p. 1164; SE p. 705): What connections are made between Williams's two professions, poet and physician? How does Berryman revise the idea of "envy" common to these elegies for poets? How do the other Dream Songs in the anthology suggest why Berryman envies less Williams's virtuosity than his being beyond the need to prove it?

E. Elegies for Animals

Do elegies for animals seem to shade into parody, the way a pet cemetery can seem to be a sick joke about graveyards? How do these poems test the limits of the conventions of the elegy? This topic might be used to lead into the next, light verse. See also Section 7.13, on animals.

Gray, "Ode: On the Death of a Favorite Cat, Drowned in a Tub of Goldfishes" (p. 462; SE p. 247)

Cowper, "Epitaph on a Hare" (p. 481; SE p. 256): What features of the poem's diction make it teeter on the edge of parody?

What features does it share with elegies for poets and loved ones?

3.16 Light Verse

Which of these poems could be labeled nonsense verse, or poetry for children, and which would be funny only to adults? In discussing what makes these poems amusing, it is good to remember that the particular techniques alone cannot be called comic, as writers of light verse use a number of devices to comic effect that are not necessarily funny in other contexts (outlandish rhymes, invented words, surprise endings).

Anonymous, "Jolly Jankin" (p. 57; SE p. 27)
Anonymous, "Get Up and Bar the Door" (p. 44)
Gray, "Ode: On the Death of a Favorite Cat, Drowned in a Tub of
    Goldfishes" (p. 462; SE p. 247)
Byron, from *Don Juan* (p. 592; SE p. 321)
Lear, Limericks, "The Owl and the Pussy-Cat" (p. 750; SE 433)
Carroll, "Jabberwocky" (p. 825; SE 481)
Gilbert, "I Am the Very Model of a Modern Major-General"
    (p. 833; SE p. 486); "When You're Lying Awake with a Dismal
    Headache" (p. 834; SE p. 487); "Titwillow" (p. 836; SE
    p. 489)
Hardy, "The Ruined Maid" (p. 847; SE p. 497)
Parker, "Résumé" (p. 1038; SE p. 626); "One Perfect Rose"
    (p. 1038; SE p. 627)
Nash, "The Cow," "Reflections on Ice-breaking" (p. 1070; SE
    p. 649), etc.
Merrill, "The Victor Dog" (p. 1282; SE p. 780): What gives this
    energetically playful poem an earnestness or allegorical tone
    that may suggest it is a rather more ambitious kind of light
    verse than other poems on this list?

A. Epigrams

Jonson, "On English Monsieur" (p. 226; SE p. 115) and "On Gut"
    (p. 227; SE p. 117)

B. Limericks

Lear, "There Was an Old Man with a Beard," "There Was an Old
    Man in a Tree," and "There Was an Old Man who Supposed"
    (p. 749; SE 433)
Nash, "Requiem" (p. 1070; SE p. 650) and Arthur" (p. 1071; SE
    p. 651)

4 PATTERNS, STRUCTURES, AND SCHEMES

4.1 Titles

The technique of naming poems is as rich and varied as other poetic devices. Often a fruitful technique in teaching any poem can be inventing, or asking the class to invent, one or two alternate titles for the poem and discussing the range of different expectations and interpretations these titles suggest. Or title one poem on the principle used to title another; for instance, what changes if we give a title like Yeats's "An Irish Airman Foresees His Death" (p. 880; SE p. 517) to Dickinson's (untitled) Poem 712, "Because I could not stop for Death—" (p. 812; SE p. 476), or Hardy's "The Darkling Thrush" (p. 846; SE p. 497)? Or use a specific, occasion-marking title like Keats's "On Sitting Down to Read *King Lear* Once Again" (p. 648; SE p. 359) as an alternative title for Donne's "The Sun Rising" (p. 206; SE p. 101), or for Herbert's "Artillery" (p. 262; SE p. 138)? What expectations are established—and which ones denied—when a poem's title includes the genre it belongs to, as in Keats's "Ode to a Nightingale"? What features of a poem may a title be unable to, or fail to, take into account? Which poems have titles that seem to make sense right from the first line? Which poems seem rather to have to earn their titles? Which titles seem to have a strong interpretive force, urging us to respond to the poem in a way dictated by the title? Which titles seem less directive to the reader? The titles of some poems, of course, such as popular ballads, become attached to poems over time for reasons of convenience. Some poems, by design or convenience, are simply labeled by their opening lines: for which peoms is such a title a useful aid to interpretation, for which is it merely a way to designate this poem as opposed to some other one? In which poems whose title is the first line does that first line take on a deeper or emblematic resonance, so that it seems to oversee or name the whole poem rather than just to initiate it? How do conventions of titling poems change over history? What sorts of titles come in and out of vogue? I have suggested some groupings of poems that share similar titles, or that seem to be titled according to similar principles.

A. Allusive Titles

What is the initial effect of titles that cite form or allude to other poems, sometimes in another language, or to other sources? How much of the context of the poem alluded to in their titles do these poems draw upon, or ask us to be familiar with?

Longfellow, "Mezzo Cammin" (p. 676; SE p. 382)
Tennyson, "Frater Ave Atque Vale" (p. 716; SE p. 412)
Dowson, "Non sum qualis eram bonae sub regno Cynarae" (p. 898; SE p. 532): Poems that borrow their titles may in turn lend titles to other works. Students may be interested, or dismayed, to learn that the title *Gone with the Wind* comes from this poem (line 13). How does the meaning (and the grammar) of the phrase change when it is extracted from Dowson's poem, where it refers to the first of a series of past conditions of the speaker: "I have . . . gone with the wind, / Flung roses . . . lost lilies," and so on?
Owen, "Dule Et Decorum Est" (p. 1037; SE p. 626)
Graves, "Down, Wanton, Down!" (p. 1051; SE p. 636)
Hecht, "'More Light! More Light!'" (p. 1236; SE p. 754)

B. Titles of Address

Often titles direct the poem to a specific hearer, reader, or audience. Other poems so addressed may not indicate it so plainly in their titles; nor do such titles necessarily exclude other audiences. A topic for a student paper toward the end of an introductory course might be a discussion of all the things "to" can mean in such titles. What does it mean to write a poem "to" someone or something? How may writing a poem *to* someone differ from writing a poem *for* someone? What is our role as audience to poems written for someone? Do such titles turn all other readers than the one addressed into eavesdroppers? Can reading such poems be like reading a letter that is not addreessed to us? Or do we necessarily stand in for the person or object such poems claim to be addressing? See also Section 5.7 Address and Apostrophe.

Chaucer, "Complaint to His Purse" (p. 50; SE p. 20)
Skelton, "To Mistress Margaret Hussey" (p. 67; SE p. 34)
Drayton, "To the Reader of These Sonnets" (p. 223; SE p. 86)
Herrick, "To the Virgins, To Make Much of Time" (p. 246; SE p. 129)
Carew, "Song. To My Inconstant Mistress" (p. 270; SE p. 144)
Bradstreet, "The Author to Her Book" (p. 324; SE p. 169)
Marvell, "To His Coy Mistress" (p. 337; SE p. 178)
Keats, "Ode to a Nightingale" (p. 660; SE p. 370)
Whitman, "To a Locomotive in Winter" (p. 781; SE p. 456)
Stevens, "To the One of Fictive Music" (p. 932; SE p. 554)
MacLeish, "You, Andrew Marvell" (p. 1030; SE p. 621)
Kinnell, "The Correspondence School Instructor Says Goodbye to His Poetry Students" (p. 1294; SE p. 788)
Silko, "Prayer to the Pacific" (p. 1402; SE p. 853)

C. Titles of Occasion

What is the effect of the peculiar specificity of titles that name a specific occasion, that place the poet in a certain place and time either at the writing of the poem or at its conception? How may such titles bring the reader's attention, from the outset, to the act of composing the poem— or simply to the fact that the poem was composed at a certain time in response to a certain moment or event? How is our reading of the poem influenced by this initial turn of our attention to the act of writing the poem? See also Section 8.5 on occasional poems.

Donne, "Good Friday, 1613. Riding Westward" (p. 219; SE p. 111)
Bradstreet, "Here Follows Some Verses upon the Burning of Our House July 10th, 1666" (p. 325; SE p. 170)
Wordsworth, "Composed upon Westminster Bridge, September 3, 1802" (p. 550; SE p. 285)
Byron, "Written After Swimming from Sestos to Abydos" (p. 588; SE p. 318)
Keats, "On Sitting Down to Read *King Lear* Once Again" (p. 648; SE p. 359)
Thomas, "A Refusal to Mourn the Death, by Fire, of a Child in London" (p. 1179; SE p. 716)

D. Titles that name, or hint at, what the poem is intended to accomplish, what task it is designed to perform

Nashe, "Litany in Time of Plague" (p. 202; SE p. 98)
Donne, "A Valediction: Forbidding Mourning" (p. 212; SE p. 105)
Jonson, "Inviting a Friend to Supper" (p. 226; SE p. 116)

E. The Grammer of Titles

Titles that are full declarative sentences: why are these so rare? Why are poem (and other) titles so rarely statements, but most often fragments of various sorts, incomplete phrases needing to be filled out by the poem? Why are the names of poems more often names of things or people than statements about what they do ("Badger," "The Rhodora," "The Prisoner"; "Mr. Flood's Party," not "Mr. Flood Gives a Party")? When poem titles include verbs, why are they often in some form of the progressive ("Inviting a Friend to Supper," "Crossing the Bar," "Crossing Brooklyn Ferry," "Sailing to Byzantium," "Spraying the Potatoes," "Boy Breaking Glass," "Naming of Parts," "Traveling through the Dark," "Waking from Sleep," "Living in Sin")?

Browning, "The Bishop Orders His Tomb at St. Praxed's Church" (p. 720; SE p. 416)

Yeats, "An Irish Airman Foresees His Death" (p. 880; SE p. 517)
Hughes, "The Negro Speaks of Rivers" (p. 1067; SE p. 648)
Spender, "I Think Continually of Those Who Were Truly Great"
    (p. 1126; SE p. 685)
Kinnell, "The Correspondence School Instructor Says Goodbye to
    His Poetry Students" (p. 1294; SE p. 788)
Atwood, "This Is a Photograph of Me" (p. 1373; SE p. 836): Is this
    title also the first line of the poem?
Raine, "A Martian Sends a Postcard Home" (p. 1397; SE p. 849)

    F. Nonpoetic Titles

Titles that seem to belong to, or are borrowed from, some other
mode of discourse than poems become more common in this
century. What changes in twentieth-century poetry does this
tendency suggest? What is the effect of giving to a poem the sort
of title usually thought more appropriate to a painting, a musical
composition, or a how-to manual?

Stevens, "Thirteen Ways of Looking at a Blackbird" (p. 932; SE
    p. 555)
Pound, "Portrait d'une Femme" (p. 959; SE p. 572)
Eliot, "Four Quartets" (p. 1013; SE p. 611)
MacLeish, "Arts Poetica" (p. 1029; SE p. 621): This title, and the
    poems on this list by Wayman and Silko, seem more apt as
    titles for commentaries about poetry, than for poems them-
    selves. In what sense do all poems share a tacit subtitle like
    "Ars Poetica" or "How to Write a Poem about the Sky [or a
    Nightingale, Love, Spring, etc.]"? How may such titles suggest
    that the line between poetry and commentary about poetry
    may not always be easy to draw?
Olson, "Variations Done for Gerald Van De Wiele" (p. 1129; SE
    p. 686)
Koch, "Variations on a Theme by William Carlos Williams"
    (p. 1253; SE p. 763)
O'Hara, "How to Get There" (p. 1286; SE p. 782)
Reed, "beware : do not read this poem" (p. 1370; SE p. 834)
Wayman, "What Good Poems Are For" (p. 1398; SE p. 850)
Silko, "How to Write a Poem about the Sky" (p. 1401; SE p. 852)

4.2 Beginnings

Like the first brushstroke on a bare canvas, that delineates what
was formerly bare space, the first line of a poem is irrevocable, a
signing of a contract. Poems may begin with the decisive opening
wedge of an exclamation, or with an offhand conversational
remark, or with a grand pronouncement. A poet may begin as

storytellers do, giving the source of what they are about to relate, or else may begin by shocking the reader into attention. The poem's first inroad on silence may be a sigh or an outcry ("Ah, Ben!"; "Out upon it!"; "Gr-r-r—there go, my heart's abhorrence!"; "Shut, shut the door, good John!"); a reprimand ("Ay, beshrew you! by my fay"; "For God's sake hold your tongue, and let me love"; "Get up! get up for shame!"; "Hence vain deluding Joys"); a question—sometimes demanding an answer and sometimes not ("Why does your brand sae drap wi' bluid?"; "How do I love thee?")—or a confession ("I, too, dislike it"; "I want a hero"). A poem may begin with a generalization or an adage that may not seem to require any proof or amplification ("All human things are subject to decay"; "Something there is that doesn't love a wall"), or with an extravagant claim or boast that seems to require the entire poem's effort to make good on ("I heard a Fly buzz—when I died—"; "How like an angel came I down!"). Or a poem can start as if it were already underway before we've started listening to it ("And then went down to the ship").

A first line can be packed, stacking the deck, presenting a formed opinion ("An old, mad, blind, despised, and dying king"; "Terence, this is stupid stuff"), or it may be hanging in mid-air, a subordinate clause promising a complex syntactic chain before the thought launched in the first line is completed ("Having been tenant long to a rich lord"; "Of man's first disobedience, and the fruit"; "since feeling is first"). A poem may begin with a report on the time and weather ("The sea is calm tonight"; "There are no stars to-night"; "I am driving; it is dusk"; "It is 12:20 in New York a Friday"; "Late summer, and at midnight"; "St. Agnes' Eve—Ah, bitter chill it was!"). Or it may set up the reader's expectations with a burst of exotic names ("In Xanadu did Kubla Khan") or familiar ones ("Just off the highway to Rochester, Minnesota").

One thing this list will suggest is that the Index in the anthology is a useful teaching tool. Assigning as a group all the poems that begin "Let . . ." is a good way to examine the range of ways a poem can invite, enjoin, seduce, and suggest. Similarly, a selection from the large group of poems that begin "I . . ." can suggest interesting ways to introduce questions of poetic persona and voice. Or reading as a group all the poems that begin with some version of an announcement of the prevailing weather (a surprisingly large group, and not just from the Romantic era, as one might expect) is one way to introduce the question of setting. Asking how a poem fulfills, alters, or breaks the promises (of tone, language, meter, subject) that its first line appears to make is something we do implicitly all the time when we invoke such categories as poetic unity or coherence. Some poets are more skilled at memorable openings than others: Dickinson, Arnold, and Lawrence are three very different poets who often begin their poems in especially striking ways. Asking a class what qualities an effective first line should have is a good way of getting them to think about broader questions concerning what kinds of things they believe poems are or should be about and how they think poems should talk about those things. Pick other lines out of poems: would they be suitable openings? What could we reasonably expect a poem that began with one of these lines to go on to say?

A related and important idea that can emerge from such questions is that we come to poems with expectations based on our experience of what kinds of things poems tend to say, and that poets depend on such readerly expectations, even if they set out to subvert them.

4.3 Middles

I don't mean to suggest by this section and the ones preceding and following it that poems are tripartite structures, but simply that it can be instructive to think of some poems as mapping for themselves an itinerary that enables them to get from the opening to the close. This journey may not be explicitly narrative, but some poems may be thought of as telling a story of their own unfolding. (See also Section 3.12, Narrative.)

An exercise may help to convince beginning students that they already read poetry with some assumptions about what a poem's progress looks like: choose a short poem, give students the first and last parts (perhaps poems in stanzas would work best), and ask them to write an approximation of what seems most likely to come between them. For which poems are students able most accurately to predict or invent the middles? For which poems is the route from beginning to end most circuitous or surprising?

Waller, "Song" (p. 274; SE p. 146): The lover's commissions to the rose work out the resemblances between the rose and the coy mistress; how does the middle stanza then stretch the bow taut to release the shaft of "Then die!" in the last stanza? Compare to the progression of argument in other seduction poems (see Section 7.16).

Bishop, "Filling Station" (p. 1139; SE p. 695): How does the poem move through a series of questions and observations from the first line's cry (of disgust?) to the last line's assured pronouncement, "Somebody loves us all"?

A. Two-Stanza Poems

Poems with only two stanzas raise the question of whether some poems do not have midles at all. An exercise: ask students to sketch out in prose a middle stanza, and consider how the insertion of this middle alters the poem's effect and meaning. You might also teach some sonnets in this context: which sonnets are conceived of in two sections, which in three or more?

Anonymous, "Western Wind" (p. 61; SE p. 29): One might make up a long story to connect the first two lines with the last two. The cryptic relation between the two halves of the poem makes this a suggestive choice for a student exercise in inserting a middle. What sort of a middle would make this poem less puzzling, and what sort might make it more puzzling?

Shakespeare, "Oh Mistress Mine" (p. 195; SE p. 93)

Campion, "When to Her Lute Corinna Sings" (p. 199; SE p. 95)

Herrick, "Upon Julia's Clothes" (p. 248; SE p. 131): The whole job is done in two stanzas: Julia dressed, Julia undressed. Would a middle stanza show us the process of Julia undressing? Why does Herrick omit this stage? (Or if this poem implies an omitted stanza, should it be a third stanza, perhaps of lovemaking?)

Blake, "The Sick Rose" (p. 505; SE p. 263) and "Ah Sun-flower" (p. 506; SE p. 264): Compare to Blake's three-stanza poems, such as "The Garden of Love" (p. 506; SE p. 265), "I Askéd a Thief" (p. 507; SE p. 265), and "Mock on, Mock on, Voltaire, Rousseau" (p. 507; SE p. 266). Does the logical development or rhetorical force of the two-stanza poems seem different from that of the three-stanza ones?

Wordsworth, "A Slumber Did My Spirit Seal" (p. 546; SE p. 281): What may be understood to have happened between the stanzas? How would the poem's effect be different if there were a middle stanza relating the woman's death?

Dickinson, Poem 49 ("I never lost as much but twice") (p. 804; SE p. 472); Poem 216 ("Safe in their Alabaster Chambers—") (p. 805; SE p. 473); Poem 305 ("The difference between Despair") (p. 808; SE p. 475); Poem 1129 ("Tell all the Truth but tell it slant—") (p. 815; SE p. 478): Which of these poems seems most as though it could accommodate a middle stanza? Which of Dickinson's three-stanza poems would suffer least, and which most, from the omission of its middle stanza? (Questions like these probably have no right answer, but in order to come up with a defensible choice, students would have to read and compare the poems with considerable care.)

Housman, "Crossing Alone the Nighted Ferry" (p. 867; SE p. 511)

Yeats, "The Scholars" (p. 881; SE p. 518)

Moore, "No Swan So Fine" (p. 987; SE p. 591)

MacDiarmid, "Empty Vessel" (p. 1026; SE p. 619)

Millay, "Above These Cares" (p. 1034; SE p. 624)

Stafford, "Accountability" (p. 1175; SE p. 713): Try reversing the order of the stanzas: how might this reversal result in a somewhat simpler poem? This exercise might be a good way to lead into the next topic, how poems end. Would Stafford's picture of a small-town winter night be more or less grim if it ended with a glance at those "bigger towns and other taverns," rather than with the image of the empty school bus? Which of the other poems on this list would still make sense if the stanzas were reversed?

Wilbur, "Boy at the Window" (p. 1222; SE p. 746)

Snyder, "Mid-August at Sourdough Mountain Lookout" (p. 1329; SE
   p. 809)
Plath, "Sleep in the Mojave Desert" (p. 1348; SE p. 820): Should the
   two sections of this poem be considered stanzas or simply verse
   paragraphs? What weight do we give to the white space
   separating the sections?

4.4 Endings

It would be useful to have an index of last lines as well as of first
ones, and not simply because for some poems we are more likely to
remember the last line than the first. Poems can end with bangs or
whimpers, with a crash of cymbals or a gentle decrescendo, with a
snappy answer, a desperate outcry, or a gentle fading of the voice.
The finality, complexity, or overall effect of a poem's ending is not
simply a product of the last line, of course; discussing poetic closure
inevitably touches upon larger matters of rhetorical development
and structure. (Barbara Herrnstein Smith's *Poetic Closure: A Study
of How Poems End* [Chicago: University of Chicago Press, 1968] is a
useful analysis of how poems end.) Poets may bring poems to an
end by breaking their pattern (particularly in a stanzaic poem that
could very well just go on and on with the addition of more stanzas),
or else by alluding to other kinds of endings or kinds of cessation
(death, sleep, night, winter).
   Bringing attention to closure can also be a way to focus a lesson
on a single poet: students may more easily notice other threads that
run through a poet's works if you ask them to look for any identifying
habits that a poet displays in ending his or her poems.

Chaucer, "Complaint to His Purse" (p. 50; SE p. 20): The closing
   "Envoy" sends the poem along to the man who could do something about the state of the poet's purse. Does this contradict
   the poet's opening claim that he is complaining only to his
   purse "and to noon other wight"?
Anonymous, "Edward" (p. 72; SE p. 35): How does the surprise
   ending suggest that the mother's long series of questions is her
   means of deferring the damning revelation about her in the last
   line?
Southwell, "The Burning Babe" (p. 163; SE p. 83): The last line's
   delayed remembrance is almost like the solving of a riddle; does
   it explain all the strange happenings in the poem?
Shakespeare, Sonnets (pp. 186-91; SE pp. 88-91): Is the aphoristic
   turn in the closing couplet sufficient to counterbalance the
   relentless mutability or despair in the first twelve lines?
   Compare to the ending of Sidney, from *Astrophel and Stella*, 1
   ("Loving in truth, and fain in verse my love to show") (p. 156;
   SE p. 80). The song "When That I Was and a Little Tiny Boy"
   (p. 195; SE p. 93) ends with a mention of the time of the
   play, bringing the poem right up to the *now* of the audience

hearing the song at the end of *Twelfth Night*. Compare the
ending of Shelley, "To a Skylark" (p. 624; SE p. 341): is the
"now" at the end our present as we read the poem, or
Shelley's (as he hears the bird? as he finishes writing his
poem about it?), or both? Compare the ending of Pope,
"Epistle to Miss Blount" (p. 423; SE p. 227).

Campion, "When Thou Must Home" (p. 199; SE p. 95): Why is the
hyperbolical accusation of the last line such a shock? When
we come to the last line, how must we revise our understanding of the rest of the poem?

Whitman. "Vigil Strange I Kept on the Field One Night" (p. 768; SE
p. 445): Why does the devastatingly blunt last line bring the
poem to such a solid ending? Because it talks about the finality
of burial? Because it is considerably shorter than any other
line in the poem?

Yeats, "Among School Children" (p. 888; SE p. 524): Yeats often
ends poems with questions, as in "The Wild Swans at Coole"
(p. 880; SE p. 516), "The Scholars" (p. 881; SE p. 518), "The
Second Coming" (p. 883; SE p. 520), "Leda and the Swan"
(p. 888; SE p. 523). See also the section on Questions (5.1).

Robinson, "Richard Cory" (p. 899; SE p. 533): The ending of the
poem is also the end of Richard Cory; compare with the
ending of Robinson's "Miniver Cheevy" (p. 900; SE p. 533),
which startles because it tells us something we did not know
about him, but which ends with a continuing, not a decisive,
terminal action (though one suspects that Miniver's drinking is
just a slow way of putting a bullet through his head).

Frost, "Stopping By Woods on a Snowy Evening" (p. 917; SE
p. 542): Why is the last line repeated? Frost excels at the
deceptively simple ending; compare "The Road Not Taken"
(p. 913; SE p. 540)— *has* the chosen road made "all the
difference" when the roads look so much alike? A decrescendo, or sense of a "diminished thing," ends not only "The
Oven Bird" (p. 914; SE p. 541) but also "Design" (p. 921; SE
p. 545), "Come In" (p. 922; SE p. 546), and "The Most of It"
(p. 923; SE p. 546).

Moore, "No Swan So Fine" (p. 987; SE p. 591): What is the effect of
the blunt, declarative clause, "The king is dead," ending a
poem characterized by sinuous, involved syntax?

Bishop, "The Fish" (p. 1136; SE p. 692): What is the effect of the
way in which the fish, and the poem about it, are "let go" in
the same moment?

Lowell, "Water" (p. 1196; SE p. 729): What is the effect of the
phrase "in the end" coming so close to the end of the poem?

Purdy, "Wilderness Gothic" (p. 1209; SE p. 738): Like the man
perched on the church spire, how is the poem left teetering
on a possibility of calamity?

Wilbur, "First Snow in Alsace" (p. 1218; SE p. 744): How does the
last line's isolation reinforce its power to end the poem? Why
do we not feel that the last line is a stanza missing its last

two lines? Among a large number of twentieth-century poems
that end with an isolated line that breaks a stanzaic pattern,
see Plath, "Ariel" (p. 1353; SE p. 823), Walcott, "The Gulf"
(p. 1333; SE p. 812), Creeley, "A Wicker Basket" (p. 1269; SE
p. 776), Wilbur, "A Storm in April" (p. 1226; SE p. 748),
Cummings, "since feeling is first" (p. 1042; SE p. 629),
MacLeish, "Calypso's Island" (p. 1031; SE p. 622), Muir, "The
Animals" (p. 991; SE p. 592), Heaney, "Mid-Term Break"
(p. 1379; SE p. 839).

Ammons, "The Put-Down Come On" (p. 1259; SE p. 768): How
does the speaker's pride in his remaining "uninformed" show
through in the sly turn to self-referential wit in the last line?
Does the last line refer to "all the time that's left" in the
poet's life or to all the time that's left in the poem?

Atwood, "Pig Song" (p. 1376; SE p. 837): The last line is almost
like a second or revised title; for other poems that end with a
surprising and bitter announcement of the poem's genre, see
Meredith, *Modern Love*, Sonnet 30 (p. 801; SE p. 469),
Hughes, "Theme for English B" (p. 1069; SE p. 648).

A. Endings That Repeat or Vary Beginnings

What is the effect of repeating (though not quite exactly) the first
line in the last? When the first line comes around again in the last,
how are we better prepared to make sense of it? Or how may our
understanding of the first line be undermined, deepened, or
qualified when it recurs in the last line? In this context, you
might also wish to teach the villanelle (Section 3.5), as a conventional pattern dictating that the poem's ending must repeat its
beginning.

Blake, "The Tyger" (p. 505; SE p. 264)
Byron, "When We Two Parted" (p. 589; SE p. 319)
Williams, "The Dance" (p. 949; SE p. 563)
Cummings, "r-p-o-p-h-e-s-s-a-g-r" (p. 1044; SE p. 631): With its
first alphabet-soup line unscrambled into "grasshopper" in the
last line, how is this poem almost a joky paradigm of this kind
of poetic closure?
MacNeice, "The Sunlight on the Garden" (p. 1112; SE p. 675)

4.5 Framed Poems

Some poems tell, or purport to tell, a story within a story, or to
begin in the words of a speaker who announces that he will
recount a second-hand report of a tale. Such framing devices put
the poem at one remove from immediacy, as well as invite
reflection on the nature of poetic narration and poetic veracity in

general. Sometimes the frames are left incomplete or unclosed—that is, the "I" who is telling the tale told to him never returns when the tale is complete, as though he became wholly absorbed in the voice whose report he is repeating ("The Two Corbies," "Ozymandias"). In other poems, the end of the poem is signaled by the conclusion of the tale-within-the-poem and by some account of the response of the original speaker to what he has heard ("The Rime of the Ancient Mariner"). Sometimes the framing narration or prologue and the tale-within-the-poem or portion within the frame will be in different meters ("On the Morning of Christ's Nativity," "Hamatreya"). See also the section on interpolated voices (5.11).

Anonymous, "The Twa Corbies" (p. 74; SE p. 37)

Coleridge, "The Rime of the Ancient Mariner" (p. 567; SE p. 298): What is the function of the poem's frame or prologue (lines 1-40) in which we learn that the Mariner's tale is narrated to the Wedding Guest? How is our reading of the entire poem colored by knowing that it is narrated to a reluctant listener who is detained from his business elsewhere? How is the frame closed at the end?

Shelley, "Ozymandias" (p. 619; SE p. 335): Why is the account of Ozymandias introduced as a second-hand report from a "traveler from an antique land"? Why does the "I" of the poem not return at the end? How would the whole poem be different if its frame were closed, that is, if it ended with something like, "And that's the story the traveler told me"?

Emerson, "Hamatreya" (p. 669; SE p. 376): How is the "Earth-song" framed by introductory and concluding material? Compare the effect of the Earth-song on the poem's speaker with the effect of the Ancient Mariner's rime on the Wedding Guest.

Tennyson, "The Lotos-Eaters" (p. 700; SE p. 398): What is the function of the introduction to the "Choric Song"? How would the poem be different if the initial voice of the storyteller were to return at the end of the Choric Song?

Yeats, "Under Ben Bulben" (p. 895; SE p. 530): In what sense does the first section, ending with "Here's the gist of what they mean" (line 12), function as a narrative or explanatory frame for the poem?

4.6 Repetition

There are many ways a poem can repeat and many things it can repeat: words, phrases, rhythms, sounds, whole stanzas. The first two sections of this Course Guide— on versification and stanza forms— are concerned with kinds of repetition basic to all poetry. Probably every poem in the anthology repeats something; this list is merely an introductory gathering to illustrate some of the kinds of reptition of words or phrases within poems, excluding refrains, which are listed below (4.8).

D'Orléans, "The Smiling Mouth" (p. 52; SE p. 22): The first two lines listing the lady's lovely features are repeated twice more in this sonnet: does the lover relieve or increase his pain by his repeated gazing and musing?
Anonymous, "I Sing of a Maiden" (p. 54; SE p. 23)
Brontë, "Remembrance" (p. 754; SE p. 435): A good introduction to a wide range of repetitive effects in poetry: have students note repeated words, phrases, sounds. How do these repetitions help to register the speaker's attitude toward remembrance?
Stevens, "Thirteen Ways of Looking at a Blackbird" (p. 932; SE p. 555)
Smith, "Poetry" (p. 1075; SE p. 652)
Silko, "How to Write a Poem about the Sky" (p. 1401; SE p. 852)

4.7 Lists and Catalogues

Poems that list things are a good way to make palpable the various kinds of organizing grids that poetic form places on words. Which of these poems seem to be taking an inventory not of things but of the words that name the things?

An exercise: have students find or make a list of fifteen or so words or items (a shopping list, ingredients in a recipe or on a package label, list of courses, list of states or presidents, chemical elements, roll of students in the class, etc.), and arrange them in five lines or so, perhaps retaining an alphabetical, chronological, or other order, and perhaps reshuffling them to bring out likenesses of sound or other similarities. How does arranging these words in lines add order, and suggest some affinities among the words or items grouped in a single line? How does arranging the words in lines also suggest increased possibilities for randomness, or new possibilities for rearrangement? Or rearrange the items catalogued in one of the poems below in some other order (alphabetical, according to number of syllables, etc.). How does the significance of the list— and of the entire listing process— change when the words are listed in a new sequence?

Nashe, "A Litany in Time of Plague" (p. 202; SE p. 98)
Herrick, "The Argument of His Book" (p. 242; SE p. 125): What is the order of items in this versified table of contents? What unifies the poem, when each line seems to have its own logic and rationale (the first line lists words that begin with "b," the second line lists the spring and summer months in order, the third lists the paraphernalia of country festivals, and so on)?

How many of the topics listed here are represented in the selections from Herrick in the anthology?

Herbert, "Prayer (I)" (p. 256; SE p. 135): Is there a discernible order to this series of analogies for, definitions of, or approximations of prayer? By the end of the poem, is the difficult, many-sided phenomenon called "prayer" at last "something understood"?

E. B. Browning, from *Sonnets from the Portuguese*: "How do I love thee? let me count the ways" (p. 674; SE p. 380)

Whitman, "Beat! Beat! Drums!" (p. 768; SE p. 446)

Gilbert, "I Am the Very Model of a Modern Major-General" (p. 833; SE p. 486)

Hopkins, "Pied Beauty" (p. 855; SE p. 503)

Stevens, "Thirteen Ways of Looking at a Blackbird" (p. 932, SE p. 555)

Parker, "Résumé" (p. 1038; SE p. 626)

Graves, "Warning to Children" (p. 635) and "The Face in the Mirror" (p. 637)

Hughes, "The Negro Speaks of Rivers" (p. 1067; SE p. 648)

Ammons, "The City Limits" (p. 1259; SE p. 769)

Kinnell, "The Correspondence School Instructor Says Goodbye to His Poetry Students" (p. 1294; SE p. 788)

Hollander, "Adam's Task" (p. 1306; SE p. 795)

4.8 Refrains

Some refrains are simply nonsense syllables enabling everyone to sing along between the stanzas (Shakespeare's "It Was a Lover and His Lass"), but others may perform a wide range of functions and have many different relations to the stanzas they punctuate or separate. A refrain may take the form of a repeated prayer or intercession (Nashe's "A Litany in Time of Plague," Kipling's "Recessional"), a statement that counters or outweighs the stanzas (the anonymous lyric "There Is a Lady Sweet and Kind"), an analogy that unites the varied matter of the individual stanzas (Yeat's "Long-Legged Fly"), a response from or the interpolation of a new voice (Hardy's "The Ruined Maid").

Some refrains accumulate significance as they recur after each stanza. Each time such a refrain comes around, how has it become richer (more resonant, more confusing, more suggestive)? Other refrains may seem to be drained of meaning through repetition.

An exercise: have students invent a refrain for a short poem in stanzas which doesn't have one; likely candidates— for different reasons— include Herrick's "To the Virgins, to Make Much of Time" (p. 246; SE p. 129), Lovelace's "To Lucasta, Going to the Wars" (p. 333; SE p. 176), Blake's "Holy Thursday [II.]" (p. 504; SE p. 262), Wordsworth's "She Dwelt Among the Untrodden Ways" (p. 545; SE p. 280), Housman's "Loveliest of Trees" (p. 861; SE

p. 506), Frost's "Come In" (p. 922; SE p. 546), and Roethke's "My Papa's Waltz" (p. 1117; SE p. 679). Or invent several different refrains for the poem, based on different models of how refrains function represented by the poems on this list.

A. A Gathering of Poems with Refrains

Anonymous, "Alison" (p. 5)
Anonymous, "Timor Mortis" (p. 58; SE p. 28)
William Dunbar, "Lament for the Makaris" (p. 62; SE p. 30)
Elizabeth I, "When I Was Fair and Young" (p. 100; SE p. 55)
Tennyson, Songs from *The Princess* (p. 705; SE p. 403)
Kipling, "Recessional" (p. 870; SE p. 513)
Yeats, "The Stolen Child" (p. 875; SE p. 514) and "Long-Legged Fly" (p. 893; SE p. 529)
Dowson, "Non sum qualis eram bonae sub regno Cynarae" (p. 898; SE p. 532)

B. Nonsense or Birdsong Refrains

Anonymous, "The Cuckoo Song" (p. 3)
Shakespeare, "When Daisies Pied" (p. 193; SE p. 91), "When That I Was and a Little Tiny Boy" (p. 195; SE p. 93)
Nashe, "Spring, the Sweet Spring" (p. 201; SE p. 97)
Burns, "Green Grow the Rashes" (p. 516; SE p. 271)
Gilbert, "Titwillow" (p. 836; SE p. 489)

C. Refrains that alter in wording with each repetition

Anonymous, "This Endris Night" (p. 55; SE p. 24)
Anonymous, "Lord Randal" (p. 71; SE p. 34)
Ralegh, "The Lie" (p. 107; SE p. 61)
Spenser, "Epithalamion" (p. 138; SEp. 68)
Campion, "My Sweetest Lesbia" (p. 198; SE p. 95)
Herrick, "Corinna's Going A-Maying" (p. 244; SE p. 127)
Herbert, "Virtue" (p. 260; SE p. 137)
Tennyson, "Mariana" (p. 698; SE p. 397), "The Splendor Falls" (p. 705; SE p. 403), "Tears, Idle Tears" (p. 705; SE p. 404)
Morris, "The Earthly Paradise" (p. 832; SE p. 485)
Hardy, "The Ruined Maid" (p. 847; SE p. 497)
Kipling, "Tommy" (p. 868; SE p. 512)
Bogan, "Song for the Last Act" (p. 1053; SE p. 638)
MacNeice, "Bagpipe Music" (p. 1113; SE p. 676)

D. Refrains that are grammatically linked to the stanza
preceding them

Chaucer, "To Rosamund" (p. 49; SE p. 19), "Truth" (p. 49; SE
p. 19), and "Complaint to His Purse" (p. 50; SE p. 20)
D'Orléans, "Oft in My Thought" (p. 53; SE p. 22)
Anonymous, "Jolly Good Ale and Old" (p. 61; SE p. 30)
Campion, "There Is a Garden in Her Face" (p. 201; SE p. 97)
Gilbert, "Titwillow" (p. 836; SE p. 489)
Paul Laurence Dunbar, "We Wear the Mask" (p. 904; SE p. 537)
Parker, "One Perfect Rose" (p. 1038; SE p. 627)

5 LANGUAGE, VOICE, AND ADDRESS

5.1 Words, Names, and Labels

Some poems reflect on their own medium—words. By ringing changes on two banal, clichéd adjectives ("nice" and "pretty"), D. H. Lawrence and Stevie Smith make them resonate with surprising meanings. The poems by Carroll, Frost, and Hollander invite speculation on how things get their names, on the power of words—that is, the power of mere arbitrary combinations of sounds—to designate, label, and differentiate one thing from another. O'Hara's day in New York City is largely a random accumulation of place names, brand names, and titles. In what ways do these poems support, deny, or qualify the position that Hass's poem formulates as "a word is elegy to what it signifies"?

Blake, "The Lamb" (p. 498; SE p. 260)
Carroll, "Jabberwocky" (p. 825; SE p. 481)
Frost, "West-running Brook" (p. 919; SE p. 543)
Lawrence, "The English Are So Nice!" (p. 955; SE p. 567)
Cummings, "my father moved through dooms of love" (p. 1045; SE p. 632)
Graves, "The Cool Web" (p. 1050; SE p. 635)
Smith, "Pretty" (p. 1075; SE p. 652)
Koch, "You Were Wearing" (p. 1251; SE p. 763)
O'Hara, "The Day Lady Died" (p. 1285; SE p. 781)
Hollander, "Adam's Task" (p. 1306; SE p. 795): Which of these invented names were formed on a "portmanteau" principle like that explained in Humpty Dumpty's Explication of "Jabberwocky" (pp. 826-27; SE pp. 482-83)?
Hass, "Meditation at Lagunitas" (p. 1386; SE p. 843)

5.2 Sounds and Onomatopoeia ("Versification," p. 1411; SE p. 863)

Related to the question of how things get their names, or of the relation of things to words, is the consideration of words as sounds, and poems as structures of sounds. Some poems insist more than others on the phonetics of poetry, or admit that just about all poetry can be produced in—or reduced to—the tongue, throat, and larynx. The question of whether words can sound like natural sounds, whether "rustle" makes a rustling sound, or "buzz" imitates the sound of bees, is much debated; students are often all too eager to detect such instances of onomatopoeia, and they are often surprised to learn that they are usually "hearing" sounds or qualities in the words only because of strong associations with the words' meanings. I find that students tend to attribute all sorts of qualities or feelings to the sounds of words that are clearly a property of the meaning of the words. An instructive trick: take a line such as Poe's notorious "The viol, the violet, and the vine" from "The City in the Sea," and get the class to agree that the line has a smooth, soothing, melodious sound, like the things it describes. Then alter the line slightly to "The vile, the violent, and the vain": can you get the class to "hear" a "nasty, corrupt, sneering" sound in the line now?

The poems in this list include poems whose sound is particularly prominent, usually through a combination of highly audible rhyme and strong rhythms (Skelton, Poe, Hopkins), and poems that invent nonsense words that make sense because of the associations of other words with similar sounds (Carroll, Hollander), or that describe sounds (Dryden, Merwin).

Skelton, "To Mistress Margaret Hussey" (p. 67; SE p. 34)
Dryden, "A Song for St. Cecilia's Day" (p. 375; SE p. 193)
Poe, "The City in the Sea" (p. 695; SE p. 394)
Tennyson, "Break, Break, Break" (p. 703; SE p. 402): It is surprising how readily students will claim to "hear" the sound of the crashing waves in this poem. To what degree is this an effect of the match of the rhythm of the poem and the rhythm of the sea-swells? To what degree is it a resemblance fostered by the meaning of the words, rather than their sound or rhythm? Revise the poem's opening to "Brook, brook, brook, / On thy smooth gray stones, O flow," and what does the repeated word "sound like"? (Or, more mischievously, "Brake, brake, brake / On thy coiled greased shocks, O Sedan . . ."). Compare imitative effects in "Dover Beach" (see "Versification," p. 1416; SE p. 858).
Arnold, "Dover Beach" (p. 794; SE p. 463)
Carroll, "Jabberwocky" (p. 825; SE p. 481)
Hopkins, "The Windhover" (p. 855; SE p. 503)
Millay, "Euclid Alone Has Looked on Beauty Bare" (p. 1033; SE p. 623): Do we "hear [Beauty's] massive sandal set on stone" in the last line?
Merwin, "The Drunk in the Furnace" (p. 1295; SE p. 789): A poem that describes a series of loud, grating sounds is a good place to investigate the question of whether the words that describe or name those sounds also echo or imitate them.
Hollander, "Adam's Task" (p. 1306; SE p. 795)

5.3 Speaker

The fiction that in a poem we hear a voice speaking is one of its most persistent and powerful devices. This list illustrates the range of voices that a poem may invent, not all of them human. For convenience in an introductory course, the poems listed here are all in the first person, but it is arguable that all poems fictionalize or create figures of voice.

Chaucer, "The Pardoner's Prologue and Tale" (p. 24; SE p. 6)

Donne, "The Relic" (p. 215; SE p. 108)

Jonson, "Though I Am Young and Cannot Tell" (p. 238; SE p. 122)

Herbert, "Affliction (I)" (p. 255; SE p. 134)

Blake, "The Little Black Boy" (p. 499; SE p. 261)

Burns, "Holy Willie's Prayer" (p. 512; SE p. 269)

Wordsworth, "Lines Composed a Few Miles above Tintern Abbey" (p. 523; SE p. 273): The speaker of this poem seems much closer to the poet, the historical Wordsworth, than the speaker of Blake's "The Little Black Boy" or of Plath's "Elm"; nonetheless what means do all these poems share to create the fiction of a voice speaking the poem?

Clare, "I Am" (p. 646; SE p. 358): Compare to Thoreau, "I Am a Parcel of Vain Strivings Tied" (p. 752; SE p. 434)

Browning, "My Last Duchess" (p. 717; SE p. 413)

Whitman, from "Song of Myself" (p. 760; SE p. 438)

Plath, "Elm" (p. 1351; SE p. 821)

5.4 Tone

Tone has to do with the attitude the speaker takes toward his own words, an attitude we as readers may or may not share, or that the poet who invented the speaker may or may not share. For which of these poems is the tone established right from the first line, for which does it take the reader somewhat longer to determine what the most likely tone of the poem as a whole should be, and in which does the tone change as the poem progresses? How does the range of available or acceptable tones or speaking attitudes widen in the twentieth century?

Chaucer, "Complaint to His Purse" (p. 50; SE p. 20)

Blake, "Holy Thursday [II.]" (p. 504; SE p. 262)

Byron, "Written After Swimming from Sestos to Abydos" (p. 588; SE p. 318)

D.G. Rossetti, "The Woodspurge" (p. 798; SE p. 467)

Meredith, *Modern Love*, 17 ("At dinner, she is hostess, I am host") (p. 801; SE p. 469)

Dickinson, Poem 216 ("Safe in their Alabaster Chambers— ") (p. 805; SE p. 473): How does the revised second stanza alter the tone of the whole poem?

C. Rosetti, "Song" (p. 817; SE p. 479)

Hardy, "Channel Firing" (p. 849; SE p. 500)

McDiarmid, "In the Children's Hospital" (p. 1027; SE p. 620)

Kavanagh, "Inniskeen Road: July Evening" (p. 1087; SE p. 659)

Bishop, "Filling Station" (p. 1139; SE p. 695)
Rich, "Orion" (p. 1313; SE p. 797)
Corso, "Marriage" (p. 1321; SE p. 804)
Raab, "Attack of the Crab Monsters" (p. 1399; SE p. 851)

5.5 Diction

A. High Poetic Diction

Formal, elaborate, strongly "poetic" language suggests ways in which poetry itself may be considered a kind of dialect, a branch of non-standard English. I have listed here a range of poems whose language is markedly "poetic," hieratic, or mannered in some way. Eighteenth-century poetry provides the most obvious examples, but the poetry of our own century has its own high styles as well. Often this high style is characterized by Latinate diction, allegorical or mythological figures, and grammatical inversions of normal word order. When would it be an insult, when a compliment, to call someone's speech or writing "poetic"?

An exercise: rewrite in high poetic style a conversational phrase, a nursery rhyme, or a short colloquial poem. For a good example of how comic the results can be, see the section on "The Buskin Style" in Pope's *Peri Bathous*, where an everyday command, "Uncork the bottle and chip the bread," is preposterously inflated into "Apply thine engine to the spongy door, / Set Bacchus from his Glassy Prison free, / And strip white Ceres of her nut-brown Coat."

Milton, "On the Late Massacre in Piedmont" (p. 293; SE p. 164)
Wilmot, "A Satire Against Mankind" (p. 385; SE p. 200)
Collins, "Ode on the Poetical Character" (p. 467; SE p. 251)
Keats, "On First Looking into Chapman's Homer" (p. 648; SE
    p. 359): Why does the diction become less heightened in the
    sonnet's sestet?
Poe, "The City in the Sea" (p. 695; SE p. 394)
D.G. Rossetti, "The Blessed Damozel" (p. 795; SE p. 464): How
    does Rossetti manage to establish a context of archaic words
    ("damozel," "herseemed") and phrasings ("And the stars in
    her hair were seven") so that even seemingly colloquial,
    straightforward usages ("yellow like ripe corn") take on a
    medieval aura or a taste of timeworn, obsolete English?
Hopkins, "[Thou Art Indeed Just, Lord . . .]" (p. 860; SE p. 506)
Dowson, "Non sum qualis eram bonae sub regno Cynarae" (p. 898;
    SE p. 532)
Stevens, "Sunday Morning" (p. 929; SE p. 551): To what degree is
    the heightened manner of this poem a matter of Latinate
    diction ("unsubdued elations," "ambiguous undulations") or a
    clash between Latinate and Anglo-Saxon words ("indifferent
    blue," "inarticulate pang"), or curious adjectives ("mythy")?

To what degree does the poem's rhetoric—the long complex sentences, the frequent questions—contribute to the elevated manner?

Lawrence, "Bavarian Gentians" (p. 956; SE p. 568)
Hill, from "Mercian Hymns' (p. 14341; SE p. 816)

B. Low or Colloquial Diction

This group of poems that feature everyday, conversational language is closely related to the topic of speaker (5.3). Which of these poems uses a colloquial style to announce, "This poem ain't got no manners," as Ishmael Reed does in "beware : do not read this poem"? To what degree are poems written in even the most simple, informal, or slangy diction and grammar marked by some "poetic" variant of the colloquial? See also the section on blank verse (1.5) for poems that attempt to reproduce or discover in iambic pentameter the everyday rhythms of English.

Skelton, "Mannerly Margery Milk and Ale" (p. 66; SE p. 33): Which of the other poems on this list get as down-to-earth in their language as Skelton does in phrases like, "I love you an whole cart-load" (line 9)?
Ralegh, "The Lie" (p. 107; SE p. 60)
Donne, "The Canonization" (p. 207; SE p. 102) and "Song" ("Sweetest love, I do not go") (p. 208; SE p. 103): Just about all of the ingredients in "The Canonization" are simple words in common usage: where then does its heightened poetic flavor come from?
Pope, "Epistle to Dr. Arbuthnot" (p. 432; SE p. 229): Compare the blunt, imperative opening of this poem ("Shut, shut the door!") to the brusque first line of Donne's "The Canonization" ("For God's sake, hold your tongue . . ."). Which poem sustains that irritated, colloquial tone more consistently? For Pope's language at its simplest, see "The Universal Prayer" (p. 430; SE p. 227).
Wordsworth, "She Dwelt Among the Untrodden Ways" (p. 545; SE p. 280) and "Resolution and Independence" (p. 546; SE p. 281)
Whitman, from "Song of Myself," 24 ("Walt Whitman, a kosmos, of Manhattan the son"): How is Whitman's boast to be the medium of ordinary "dumb voices" undercut by his occasional use of heightened diction ("afflatus," line 50; "gambols," line 553) and poetically inverted word order ("the password primeval," line 506; "Voices indecent by me clarified," line 518)? Or are such elevated expressions counterbalanced by the blunt, unembarrassed inclusion of such words as "armpits" (line 525) and "dung" (line 515)? Does "dung" seem more polite when Swift uses it in "A Description of a City Shower," (p. 393; SE p. 207, line 61)?

Frost, "The Most of It" (p. 923; SE p. 546)

Cummings, "'next to of course god america i'" (p. 1042; SE p. 629): Cummings enables us to hear a frightening strain of American talk: the inflated rhetoric of knee-jerk patriotism sounds even emptier beside the self-congratulatory, complacent slang. What is the effect of the snatches of songs mixed in with such vernacular expressions as those piled up in line 8? How does the poem's last line underscore the phony theatricality of the orator's performance?

Miles, "Reason" (p. 1144; SE p. 698): What marks this speaker's lingo as American? Compare to Cummings, "'next to of course god america i.'"

Simic, "The Partial Explanation" (p. 1372; SE p. 835): Compare to Miles's "Reason": what is the effect of omitting the first word of the sentences in these two poems?

5.6 Dialect

Poems in Scots, or black English, or some other marked dialect bring to our attention that all poets write in some dialect of English—usually the dominant dialect that we call standard English, unmindful that it is standard only because the limited class of people who speak it assume or declare that it is. You might wish to include some of these poems in dialect in connection with the poems with first-person speakers (5.3). For poems with a similar colloquial informality, see Section 5.5.B.

Burns, "To a Mouse" (p. 511; SE p. 268); "Holy Willie's Prayer" (p. 512; SE p. 269)

Dunbar, "Little Brown Baby" (p. 904; SE p. 537): Couched in black dialect, how does the father's wish that his baby could stay a child (line 31) hint at what life is like for those whose way of speaking English is part of what marks and enforces their marginal status in the dominant society?

Lawrence, "The English Are So Nice!" (p. 955; SE p. 567): This poem suggests that Lawrence heard the polite, empty speech of the English as, in effect, an excluding and elitist dialect.

Eliot, "The Waste Land," lines 139-172 (p. 1004; SE p. 603): Among the many voices of the poem, you might single out this section in Cockney slang; you might also ask students to locate passages in "The Waste Land" that imitate the precious overpolite English manner spoofed in Lawrence's "The English Are So Nice!"

MacDiarmid, "The Watergaw" (p. 1025; SE p. 619); "Empty Vessel" (p. 1026; SE p. 619)

5.7 Address and Apostrophe

Various modes of address, often marked by the device of apostrophe, are a traditional and central device in some poetic genres. Most odes will include some moments in which the subject of the ode is directly addressed or invoked: the breathless "Thou"s and "Oh"s of the Romantic ode can seem to make apostrophizing hard work. Elegies, too, conventionally speak to the dead person, and often as well use apostrophe in calling upon other people, or mythological creatures, for consolation. Epics begin by apostrophizing or invoking the muse, and apostrophes may call upon some animating spirit to enter the poet or to come to him. This list attempts to illustrate the variety of things poets will apostrophize— the muse, a rose, the sea, the wind. See the section on Titles for a listing of poems that are titled *to* someone or something. Apostrophe can be problematic when we try to imagine poems as the utterances of hypothetical speakers (see Section 5.3), since it is hard to imagine in just what circumstances, outside of a poem, a speaker would talk directly to a lute, a nightingale, a rose, the wind, etc. For an illuminating discussion of this and of other difficulties posed by apostrophe, see Jonathan Culler, "Apostrophe," *The Pursuit of Signs* (Ithaca, N.Y.: Cornell University Press, 1980).

Anonymous, "The Cuckoo Song" (p. 3; SE p. 3)
Anonymous, "Weep You No More, Sad Fountains" (p. 88; SE p. 48): What is the effect of the shift from "sad fountains" to "sad eyes" as the object of the apostrophe? Compare Jonson's "Slow, Slow, Fresh Fount" (p. 237; SE p. 121).
Wyatt, "My Lute, Awake!" (p. 92; SE p. 51): How is the apostrophe to the lute almost like an apostrophe, within the poem, to the poem itself as it proceeds?
Sidney, "The Nightingale" (p. 154; SE p. 79): Why does each stanza begin by describing the nightingale, and then apostrophize it with "O Philomela fair"?
Shakespeare, "Blow, Blow, Thou Winter Wind" (p. 194; SE p. 92)
Wotton, "On His Mistress, the Queen of Bohemia" (p. 203; SE p. 99)
Donne, "The Sun Rising" (p. 206; SE p. 101)
Herbert, "Virtue" (p. 260; SE p. 137)
Waller, "Song" ("Go, lovely rose!") (p. 274; SE p. 146)
Milton, "L'Allegro" (p. 284; SE p. 156); "Il Penseroso" (p. 287; SE p. 159): Why do both these poems begin with apostrophes to a caricatured, extreme, allegorical version of the state of mind they wish to banish?
Lovelace, "The Grasshopper" (p. 334; SE p. 176)
Vaughan, "They Are All Gone into the World of Light!" (p. 350; SE p. 186): The opening meditation on departed friends might lead us to expect that the poet would invoke those friends; why do we instead get apostrophes to "holy hope, and high

humility" (line 13), "Dear, beauteous death" (line 17), and
"Father of eternal life" (line 33)?

Gray, "Ode: On the Death of a Favorite Cat, Drowned in a Tub of
Goldfishes" (p. 462; SE p. 247)

Byron, "On This Day I Complete My Thirty-sixth Year" (p. 612; SE
p. 333): What is the function of the self-correction or self-
clarification of who or what is being commanded to "Awake!"
in lines 25-26?

Shelley, "Ode to the West Wind" (p. 620; SE p. 337)

Tennyson, "Break, Break, Break" (p. 703; SE p. 402)

Whitman, "Crossing Brooklyn Ferry" (p. 764; SE p. 442)

Arnold, "The Scholar-Gypsy" (p. 783; SE p. 458): This poem begins with an apostrophe to the long-deceased Scholar-Gypsy,
and almost seems to create his ghostly presence by repeatedly
addressing him. But matters get particularly interesting
around lines 231ff.: why does the speaker invoke the Scholar-
Gypsy only to warn him to keep away from the invoker and
"this strange disease of modern life" (line 203)?

Hopkins, "The Habit of Perfection" (p. 854; SE p. 501): Is there a
contradiction in an apostrophe to Silence?

Yeats, "Sailing to Byzantium" (p. 886; SE p. 523): What is the effect
of delaying the apostrophe of the "sages" until the third
stanza?

Stevens, "The Idea of Order at Key West" (p. 934; SE p. 557): Why
does the speaker address "Ramon Fernandez" in line 44?

Jeffers, "Shine, Perishing Republic" (p. 981; SE p. 588): Compare
the final address to "boys" (line 9) with the advice addressed
to "ye beauties" in the last stanza of Gray's "Ode to the Death
of a Favorite Cat."

Eliot, "The Dry Salvages" (p. 1013; SE p. 611): How can we account
for the endurance of the musty old device of apostrophe, even
into high modernism? What is the effect of the apostrophe in
lines 162ff.?

Toomer, "Georgia Dusk" (p. 1048; SE p. 634): Does the direct
address to the singers in the last stanza seem a natural out-
growth of the poem's development?

5.8 Questions

Poems that ask questions, or are occasioned by a question, generally set out to do more than provide answers. This topic may be
usefully linked to apostrophe (Section 5.7), since often the poet
asks a question directly of the subject that he addresses. When a
question recurs in a refrain, how may the intervening stanzas, by
refusing or delaying an answer, lend it an added urgency? Why are
love poems (Sidney, Wotton, Donne) so often structured upon a
series of questions? How does the centrality of questions in both
love poetry and religious poetry suggest deeper affinities between
these topics?

Anonymous, "Ubi Sunt Qui Ante Nos Fuerunt?" (p. 3; SE p. 3):
Compare to the opening of Klein's "Indian Reservation:
Caughnawaga" (p. 1124; SE p. 684).
Anonymous, "Western Wind" (p. 61; SE p. 29)
Anonymous, "Lord Randal" (p. 71; SE p. 34) and "Edward" (p. 72;
SE p. 35)
Sidney, from Astrophel and Stella, 31 ("With how sad steps, Oh
Moon, thou climb'st the skies") (p. 157; SE p. 80) and 47
("What, have I thus betrayed my liberty?") (p. 157; SE p. 81)
Shakespeare, Sonnet 146 ("Poor soul, the center of my sinful
earth") (p. 191; SE p. 91)
Wotton, "On His Mistress, the Queen of Bohemia" (p. 203; SE p. 99)
Donne, "Woman's Constancy" (p. 206; SE p. 101)
Jonson, "On English Monsieur" (p. 226; SE p. 115)
Herbert, "Jordan (I)" (p. 256; SE p. 136)
Carew, "A Song" (p. 269; SE p. 143): How does the speaker's
repeated refusal to be questioned act as a substitution for a
question?
Suckling, "Song" (p. 317; SE p. 166)
Blake, "The Tyger" (p. 505; SE p. 264) and "The Lamb" (p. 498; SE
p. 260)
Shelley, "Ode to the West Wind" (p. 620; SE p. 337): What is the
effect of a question coming at the end of a poem characterized
throughout by exclamations and imperatives? Compare to
the shifts from exclamations to questions and back again in
Shelley's "To a Skylark" (p. 624; SE p. 341).
Keats, "Ode on a Grecian Urn" (p. 663; SE p. 372) and "Ode to a
Nightingale" (p. 660; SE p. 370): What larger differences between these two odes are suggested when we note that "Urn"
moves through a series of questions to end with an epigrammatic pronouncement, while "Nightingale" moves through
exclamations and pronouncements ("Already with thee!")
to end with a question? Compare the questions in "To
Autumn" (p. 664; SE p. 99)—do that ode's questions seem easier
to answer, or less in need of an answer?
Emerson, "The Rhodora" (p. 666; SE p. 375): What besides the
subtitle, "On being asked, whence is the flower?", suggests that
this poem is an answer to a question? Compare the method and
range of Emerson's answer to "whence is the flower?" to
Whitman's answer to "What is the grass?" in "Song of Myself"
(Section 6). Is "whence" a narrower question than "what"?
E.B. Browning, "Sonnets from the Portuguese," 43 ("How do I love
thee? Let me count the ways") (p. 674; SE p. 380)
Poe, "Sonnet—To Science"¯ (p. 694; SE p. 393)
Whitman, from "Song of Myself," 6 ("A child said What is the
grass?") (p. 760; SE p. 438): Why doesn't Whitman use Blake's
method and ask the question directly of the grass itself ("Oh,
grass, what are you?"? Compare with Sandburg, "Grass"
(p. 926; SE p. 549), where the grass is the speaker.

Language, Voice, and Address / 67

De la Mare, "The Listeners" (p. 906; SE p. 538): Compare Frost's
"The Most of It" (p. 923; SE p. 546), where again a question,
or some articulate call for a response, is sent out into a
space that is unresponding, or responds in an unexpected
way.
Frost, "Design" (p. 921; SE p. 545)
Dickey, "In the Tree House at Night" (p. 1233; SE p. 752)
Corso, "Marriage" (p. 1321; SE p. 804)
Baraka, "In Memory of Radio" (p. 1356; SE p. 827)

5.9 Letters

Poems that take the form of letters addressed from one person to
another raise in direct and easily grasped terms the way a poem
may be a circuit of communication. Since the poem must on some
level also be addressed to us, the reader, we can compare the ways
that these poems serve the needs of both the private and public
audience. How is reading poems like reading someone else's mail,
with the accompanying thrills and hazards of overhearing a
communication not addressed to us?

Bradstreet, "A Letter to Her Husband, Absent Upon Public Employ-
ment" (p. 324; SE p. 170)
Pope, "Epistle to Miss Blount" (p. 423; SE p. 226)
Williams, "This Is Just to Say" (p. 945; SE p. 562): In teaching this
poem in any context, it is useful to bring in Kenneth Koch's
sly parodies of it, "Variations on a Theme by William Carlos
Williams" (p. 1253; SE p. 763)
Pound, "The River-Merchant's Wife: a Letter" (p. 963; SE p. 575)
Raine, "A Martian Sends a Postcard Home" (p. 1397; SE p. 849)

5.10 Dialogue

Poems structured around the exchange of two or more speakers
may illustrate a range of rhetorical effects: the dialogue may be an
outright debate or argument (as in the poems listed below by
Sidney and Daniel) or a static pair of statements of each speaker's
position on a matter about which they are too opposed even to
debate (Blake, Ransom). In some poems one speaker seems to act
as straight man setting up the other's punchlines, or as a mere
interlocutor giving the main speaker an opportunity to hold forth
(Pope, Yeats, Frost); in other poems, one speaker asks questions
and another gives answers (Popular Ballads, "As You Came from the
Holy Land," Rossetti, Housman). These poems may serve to introduce such forms as the ode, in which one stanza may respond to

another in a muted or implied dialogue (Wordsworth, "Ode: Intimations of Immortality," p. 551; SE p. 286), or the sonnet, many of which might be taught as a dialogue of alternate voices or points of view (Shakespeare, Sonnet 65, p. 188; SE p. 89). A consideration of which voice tends to get the last word in poetic dialogues (or in odes and sonnets) links this schematic grouping to the topic of closure.

Popular Ballads: "Lord Randal" (p. 71; SE p. 34); "Edward" (p. 72; SE p. 35); "The Unquiet Grave" (p. 75; SE p. 39)
Sidney, "Ye Goatherd Gods" (p. 153; SE p. 77)
Daniel, "Ulysses and the Siren" (p. 166; SE p. 84)
Anonymous, "As You Came from the Hold Land of Walsingham" (p. 85; SE p. 46)
Herbert, "Love (III)" (p. 268; SE p. 141)
Suckling, "Upon My Lady Carlisle's Walking in Hampton Court Garden" (p. 318; SE p. 166)
Pope, "Epistle to Dr. Arbuthnot" (p. 432; SE p. 229)
Blake, "The Clod and the Pebble" (p. 504; SE p. 263): Compare to other dialogues about love, Herbert's "Love (III)," and Suckling's "Upon My Lady Carlisle's Walking." On the topic of love, which speaker in these poems might be said to take the part of clod (love is selfless and uplifting) and which of pebble (love is selfish, envious, and demeaning)?
C. Rossetti, "Up-Hill" (p. 819; SE p. 480)
Hardy, "The Ruined Maid" (p. 847; SE p. 497)
Housman, "Is My Team Plowing?" (p. 863; SE p. 1508)
Yeats, "Adam's Curse" (p. 879; SE p. 516)
Frost, "West-running Brook" (p. 919; SE p. 543): Compare the woman"s role in this dialogue and in Yeats, "Adam's Curse."
Ransom, "Piazza Piece" (p. 1019; SE p. 616)
Miles, "Reason" (p. 1144; SE p. 698): Is one speaker recounting an incident chiefly in terms of what each person involved said?
Bukowski, "vegas" (p. 1212; SE p. 740)

5.11 Cited or Interpolated Voices

A number of poems include as a central fiction the words of another voice. Some of these may be best taught in conjunction with poems that stage a dialogue, or with poems that are framed by an introductory setting or are told as tales-within-a-tale (see the section on framed poems, 4.5). It may be useful to try to distinguish between poems in which this second voice seems to interpose itself willfully, and those in which it is invited into the poem.

Milton, "Lycidas" (p. 275; SE p. 147): What is the function of the series of voices, heard from one or many lines (Phoebus, Neptune, Camus, St. Peter)? See also Milton's "When I Consider How My Light Is Spent" (p. 293; SE p. 164), where the voice of "Patience" completes the poem.

Coleridge, "The Rime of the Ancient Mariner" (p. 567; SE p. 308): How many different voices do we hear in this poem? Should we distinguish the voice of the narrator from the voice of the marginal annotations? In what ways does the dialogue between the First Voice and the Second Voice at the beginning of Part VI resemble the reader's voice questioning the poem and the poem (or the narrator?) replying?

D.G. Rossetti, "The Blessed Damozel" (p. 795; SE p. 464): Are the voice of the speaker, the voice of the Blessed Damozel, and the voice who speaks inside parentheses best read as three separate voices?

Whitman, "Out of the Cradle Endlessly Rocking" (p. 770; SE p. 446): What is the relation between the voice of the bird and the voice that speaks the poem? between both and the voice of the sea?

Eliot, "The Waste Land" (p. 1000; SE p. 599): The poem is a veritable choir of many different voices, quoted, invented, ventriloquized: one way of teaching the poem is to investigate the varieties and development of these voices, from the Dantean words of the poem's dedication to the voice of Tiresias (lines 215ff.), from the barroom Cockney of lines 139-172 (which ends with lines of Ophelia) to the voice of the thunder speaking words from the Upanishads.

Larkin, "Myxomatosis" (p. 1229; SE p. 750): What is the effect of the imagined voice of the diseased rabbit in line 3?

6 FIGURATIVE LANGUAGE

6.1 Introducing Figurative Language

Figurative language in poetry is, of course, an enormous topic, and a pervasive one. Most of a poetry course is concerned, on some level, with the ways poems say one thing in terms of another, compare or juxtapose things, or give things a new slant through some kind of gesture that we might call figurative. Some of the poems listed bring into focus the issue of figurative language because they hang on a single striking metaphor or comparison (Tennyson, Williams, Merwin). Others listed below may serve as an introduction to questions of figuration because they take figures of speech as their topic, or explicitly weigh the aptness of metaphors (Shakespeare, Dickinson). or because they propose a shifting series of likenesses (Burns, Shelley, Keats).

Shakespeare, Sonnet 18, "Shall I compare thee to a summer's day"
(p. 186; SE p. 88): Perhaps most fruitfully taught in
conjunction with the witty rejection of the Petrarchan
comparisons in Sonnet 130, "My mistress' eyes are nothing
like the sun" (p. 190; SE p. 90).

Burns, "A Red, Red Rose" (p. 522; SE p. 273): A good poem to
remind students that we understand how to read many
metaphors because of conventional associations with the
objects that serve as their vehicles. How, for example, do we
know that when Burns compares a woman to a rose he is not
saying that she has thorns or petals but that she is beautiful
and transient? What might a poet have to do to include or
emphasize those other features of the rose in the comparison?

Shelly, "To a Skylark" (. 624; SE p. 341)

Keats, "On First Looking into Chapman's Homer" (p. 658; SE
p. 359)

Tennyson, "Crossing the Bar" (p. 716; SE p. 412)

Henry David Thoreau, "I Am a Parcel of Vain Strivings Tied"
(p. 752; SE p. 434)

Arnold, "The Scholar-Gypsy" (p. 783; SE p. 458): Note the final
extended metaphor of the "Tyrian-trader" (lines 232ff.): what
is the effect of this sudden opening up of the poem to the
world beyond the landscape around Oxford?

Dickinson, Poem 1129: "Tell all the Truth but tell it slant—"
(p. 815; SE p. 478): A classic statement of the rationale for
metaphor, this poem itself offers a series of comparisons for
the poetic act of making comparisons.

Yeats,"Long-legged Fly" (p. 893; SE p. 527): The refrain gives us
three chances to test the aptness of the metaphor, and to
refine our sense of the ground of the comparison: Caesar,

form certain (mental) actions in the way a certain kind of fly performs a certain action.

Williams, "To Waken an Old Lady" (p. 944; SE p. 561)

"Queen-Ann's-Lace" (p. 945; SE p. 561)

Pound, "In a Station of the Metro" (p. 963; SE p. 575)

Cummings, "somewhere i have never travelled,gladly beyond" (p. 1043; SE p. 630): A good class discussion on metaphor might center around the difference between Burns's "my love's like a red, red rose" and Cummings's more riddling comparison, "the voice of your eyes is deeper than all roses" (line 19).

Bly, "Waking from Sleep" (p. 1267; SE p. 774)

Merwin, "Separation" (p. 1296; SE p. 790): This and the Atwood poem are a good pair to start with, as both very briefly give to a conventional comparison an unexpected twist.

Cohen, "As Mist Leaves No Scar" (p. 1360; SE p. 828)

Atwood, "You Fit into Me" (p. 1375; SE p. 837)

6.2 Riddles

Riddles can be a useful category for introducing figurative language. Saying one thing in terms of another, or in unfamiliar, novel ways often involves the reader in a game of guessing the comparison.

Anonymous, "I Sing of a Maiden" (p. 54; SE p. 23): The riddle or paradox of a woman who is simultaneously "mother and maiden" suggests that riddles, or the paradoxes they represent, are central to the language of religious poetry.

Anonymous, "I Have a Young Sister" (p. 56; SE p. 25): Why do the first three riddels turn on a solution involving a nascent or undeveloped stage of growth, while the fourth involves a state of fulfillment or completion?

Tichborne, "Tichborne's Elegy" (p. 105; SE p. 58): How does this series of metaphors for an early death become increasingly paradoxical and riddling?

Dickinson, Poem 986 ("A narrow Fellow in the Grass" (p. 814; SE p. 477): Like a riddle, the poem lists the attributes of the creature (a snake) but does not name him, as does Poem 1463 ("A Route of Evanescence") (p. 816; SE p. 478), a more oblique description of a humming bird.

C. Rossetti,"Up-Hill" (p. 819; SE p. 480): Almost in riddle format of question and answer, the solution becomes clearer as the questions accumulate. In what sense is death itself a riddle?

Raine, "A Martian Sends a Postcard Home" (p. 1397; SE p. 849): Commonplace objects seen through the eyes of a creature alien to earth lead to riddling descriptions. When does the Martian's puzzled report accurately tell what life on earth is like?

6.3 Allegory and Personification

Nowadays we tend to feel that the device of giving abstract qualities human or personified attributes is somewhat clunky or old-fashioned, the stuff of greeting cards or advertisements, where allegorical personages standing for products or their qualities still reign supreme. But as a shorthand procedure for talking about the conflicts of values or the growth of ideas, these devices have remained effective, although in somewhat attenuated forms, up to the present day (you might wish to discuss with the class to what degree the same logic governs the invention of an allegorical figure of, say, Cleanliness or Purity, and of such commercial characters as Mr. Clean or even Miss America). Allegorical personages are often pictured with emblematic props or as holding a characteristic pose: Collins's "Truth, in sunny vest arrayed" ("Ode on the Poetical Character," line 45); Keats's "Joy, whose hand is ever at his lips / Bidding adieu" ("Ode on Melancholy"); Emerson's "Days . . . marching single in an endless file"; Swinburne's "Time, with a gift of tears"). You might have students invent the appropriate accoutrements and poses for some contemporary, minor, or little recognized virtues and vices (such as Neatness, Lateness, Consistency, Inefficiency).

Spenser, from *The Faerie Queene* Book V, Canto II (p. 131; SE p. 62)
Ralegh, "Ring Out Your Bells" (p. 155; SE p. 79)
Sidney, from *Astrophel and Stella*, 52 ("A strife is grown between Virtue and Love") (p. 158; SE p. 82)
Daniel, from "*Delia*", 6 ("Fair is my love, and cruel as she's fair") (p. 165; SE p. 83): What is lost if lines 9-10 are rewritten to eliminate the personifications? What is the difference between calling Chastity and Beauty "deadly foes" and calling them simply opposed principles, or contradictory values?
Boyd, "Fra Bank to Bank" (p. 168; SE p. 86)
Jonson, "Though I Am Young and Cannot Tell" (p. 238; SE p. 122)
Milton, "On the Morning of Christ's Nativity" (p. 278; SE p. 151) and "On Shakespeare" (p. 291; SE p. 163): Allegory can be an occasional effect as well as an overarching mode of presentation, as when Milton gives Shakespeare an allegorical ancestry, "son of Memory, great heir of Fame" (line 5). Compare to other allegorical genealogies, such as the opening of Keats's "Ode on a Grecian Urn" (p. 663; SE p. 372), or of Poe's "Sonnet—To Science" (p. 694; SE p. 393).
Johnson, "The Vanity of Human Wishes" (p. 451; SE p. 241): Several passages accumulate heaps of capitalized abstract nouns that seem to hover between allegorical embodiments of the qualities named ("captive Science" [line 144], "misty Doubt" [line 146], "hissing Infamy" [line 342] and simple descriptions of those qualities ("afflicted Worth" [line 310], "neglected Virtue" [line 333]).
Collins, "Ode on the Poetical Character" (p. 467; SE p. 251)

Keats, "Ode on Melancholy" (p. 662; SE p. 371): What is the effect of the increased population of personified qualities (Beauty, Joy, Pleasure, Delight, Melancholy) in the last stanza?

Poe, "Sonnet—To Science" (p. 694; SE p. 393)

Emerson, "Days" (p. 674; SE p. 379)

Arnold, "The Scholar-Gypsy" (p. 783; SE p. 458): Compare the figure of "close-lipped patience" (line 194) with "Patience" who speaks in Milton's "When I Consider How My Light Is Spent" (p. 293; SE p. 164, line 8). Should Arnold's "patience" be considered a proper instance of allegory or personification?

C. Rossetti, "Up-Hill" (p. 819; SE p. 480)

Swinburne, "Choruses from Atalanta in Calydon" (p. 837; SE p. 490)

Yeats, "The Second Coming" (p. 883; SE p. 520)

De. la Mare, "The Listeners" (p. 906; SE p. 538)

Rich, "Diving into the Wreck" (p. 1315; SE po. 798): Compare to the selections from Spenser's *Faerie Queene*: what devices do Rich and Spenser share in describing in considerable detail a difficult quest which is nonetheless clearly a spiritual one?

7 TOPICS IN THE POEMS

7.1 Poetry

Every poem, of course, espouses its own implicit *ars poetica*; these poems explicitly take up the topic of the poetic imagination. See also the sections on the Muse (7.2) and on Elegies for Poets (3.15.D).

Shakespeare, Sonnet 55 ("Not marble, nor the gilded monuments") (p. 184; SE p. 89): Do twentieth-century poets continue to uphold this sonnet's claim for the immortalizing powers of poetry?

Herbert, "Jordan (I)" (p. 256; SE p. 136)

Collins, "Ode on the Poetical Character" (p. 467; SE p. 251)

Morris, "The Earthly Paradise" (p. 832; SE p. 485): What is the effect of the poem's opening disclaimers about the power of poetry? Which of the poems in this group would attribute to poetry some of the effects and purposes Morris dismisses in the opening stanza?

Housman, "'Terence, This Is Stupid Stuff . . .'" (p. 865; SE p. 510)

Yeats, "The Circus Animals' Desertion" (p. 894; SE p. 529)

Stevens, "The Poems of Our Climate" (p. 935; SE p. 558): Compare to Stevens's "Anecdote of the Jar" (p. 931; SE p. 554): In what sense does a poem "simplify" or "take dominion" over its surroundings, according to Stevens?

Moore, "Poetry" (p. 986; SE p. 590): What is the "raw material of poetry," according to this poem? In what sense might the short quotations Moore weaves into the poem be considered "raw material"? What might Ammons or Silko consider poetry's "raw material"?

MacLeish, "Ars Poetica" (p. 1029; SE p. 621)

Enright, "The Typewriter Revolution" (p. 1215; SE p. 741)

Ammons, "Corsons Inlet" (p. 1255; SE p. 765); "Poetics" (p. 1258; SE p. 768): To what degree does "Corsons Inlet" follow the poetic program outlined in "Poetics"? In what way could "Corsons Inlet" be titled or subtitled "Poetics"?

Ashbery, "Paradoxes and Oxymorons" (p. 1292; SE p. 787)

Hughes, "The Thought-Fox" (p. 1323; SE p. 806)

Wayman, "What Good Poems Are For" (p. 1398; SE p. 850): What range of implications does Wayman attach to the comparison between poems and house plants? Does the anecdote of the man in the bar support, qualify, or undercut that comparison?

Silko, "How to Write a Poem about the Sky" (p. 1401; SE p. 852)

7.2 The Muse

If we define a muse as any female figure whom the poet invokes or to whom he pleads for inspiration and guidance, we will find that the myth of the muse persists from the earliest poetry to the present day. Must a muse be female? Can woman poets have a muse? Anne Bradstreet in "The Author to Her Book" calls her poetry her "offspring"; do male poets also think of their poems as children they have borne? Compare Jonson's "On My First Son," in which he calls his son "his best piece of poetry" (p. 224; SE p. 115). This topic is related to questions of occasion; that is, to the larger issues of what occasions a poem, brings it into existence, or motivates the poet to write it.

Gascoigne, "Gascoigne's Lullaby" (p. 101; SE p. 57): What womanly power of voice does Gascoigne wish to claim for himself? Compare Bradstreet's comparison of her book with a child in "The Author to Her Book," and Sidney's description of himself as "great with child to speak" in the next poem.

Sidney, from *Astrophel and Stella*, 1 ("Loving in truth, and fain in verse my love to show") (p. 156; SE p. 80): Has Sidney followed his muse's advice in the writing of this poem?

Milton, from *Paradise Lost*, Book I [The Invocation] (p. 295; SE p. 165)

Bradstreet, "The Author to Her Book" (p. 324; SE p. 169): Compare the "Envoi" to Pound's "Hugh Selwyn Mauberley" (p. 964; SE p. 583)

Wordsworth, "The Solitary Reaper" (p. 559; SE p. 292)

Whitman, "Out of the Cradle" (p. 770; SE p. 446)

Stevens, "The Idea of Order at Key West" (p. 934; SE p. 556) and "To the One of Fictive Music" (p. 932; SE p. 554)

Williams, "The Young Housewife" (p. 944; SE p. 560): Compare to Wordsworth's "The Solitary Reaper": In both poems a mobile man pauses to absorb the inspiring spectacle of a woman more or less rooted to the spot, and then passes out of sight of her. Why is it important that the woman does not know she is the object of his gaze, or the subject of his poem?

Merwin, "The Drunk in the Furnace" (lp. 1295; SE p. 789): In what sense might the drunk be considered a muse figure? How is he like the singing reaper in Wordsworth's poem?

7.3 Tributes to Poets

In these poems tribute is paid by one poet to an earlier poet, in some cases one who could not have been a friend or contemporary. Compare these poems to the Elegies for Poets (Secton 3.16.D).

How is the eulogist's task different from the elegist's—that is, when what is at stake is not, as in an elegy, finding consolation for a personal loss, but declaring a poetic heritage?

Collins, "Ode on the Poetical Character" (p. 467; SE p. 251): Why does this ode, which begins with a worshipful nod to Spenser, end up as a tribute to Milton? How does Collins use Spenser to help praise Milton?

Coleridge, "On Donne's Poetry" (p. 585; SE p. 315): Compare Coleridge's figures for Donne's intricately figurative poetry to the praise of Donne's style in Carew's elegy for Donne (p. 272; SE p. 144).

Keats, "On Sitting Down to Read *King Lear* Once Again" (p. 648; SE p. 359); "To Homer" (p. 649; SE p. 360)

Arnold, "Shakespeare" (p. 782; SE p. 457): Compare the kinds of wisdom Arnold and Keats attribute to Shakespeare. Unlike Jonson's and Milton's tributes to Shakespeare, these nineteenth-century poems do not treat Shakespeare chiefly as a dramatist—there's a lesson here about how views of a poet's canon and achievements may change over time.

Hayden, "Paul Laurence Dunbar" (p. 1161; SE p. 703)

7.4 War

The poems on this list touch on many aspects of war: saber-rattling preparatory patriotism (Whitman's "Beat! Beat! Drums!", Cummings's "next to of course god"); the daily life of the soldier (Kipling, Rosenberg, Owen, Reed); the death of individual soldiers (Hardy's "Drummer Hodge," Yeats, Cummings, Jarrell); the aftermath of the slaughter (Collins, Melville, Whitman's "Vigil Strange," Sandburg, Tate); war's effect, or lack of it, on the home front (Levertov). Curiously, the actual conflict itself seems rarely to be a poetic subject: how would you account for this?

Lovelace, "To Lucasta, Going to the Wars" (p. 333; SE p. 176): Compare to Kipling, "Tommy": what do both poems suggest about the romantic illusions or social pressures that send young men to war?

Collins, "Ode Written in the Beginning of the Year 1746" (p. 467; SE p. 251)

Emerson, "Ode (Inscribed to W.H. Channing)" (p. 670; SE p. 377)

Melville, "Shiloh" (p. 758; SE p. 437)

Whitman, "Vigil Strange I Kept on the Field One Night" (p. 768; SE p. 445); "Beat! Beat! Drums!" (p. 768; SE p. 446)

Hardy, "Drummer Hodge" (p. 845; SE p. 496); "Channel Firing" (p. 849; SE p. 500)

Kipling, "Tommy" (p. 868; SE p. 512); "Recessional" (p. 870; SE p. 513)

Yeats, "The Irish Airman Foresees His Death" (p. 880; SE p. 517)

Sandburg, "Grass" (p. 926; SE p. 549)
Rosenberg, "Break of Day in the Trenches" (p. 1022; SE p. 618);
    "Louse Hunting" (p. 1023; SE p. 618)
Owen, "Strange Meeting" (p. 1035; SE p. 624); "Anthem for
    Doomed Youth" (p. 1036; SE p. 625); "Dulce et Decorum Est"
    (p. 1037; SE p. 626)
Cummings, "next to of course god america i" and "i sing of Olaf
    glad and big" (p. 1042; SE p. 629)
Tate, "Ode to the Confederate Dead" (p. 1065; SE p. 645)
Eberhart, "The Fury of Aerial Bombardment" (p. 1085; SE
    p. 659): Compare Hardy, "Channel Firing" (p. 849; SE p. 500).
Jarrell, "The Death of the Ball Turret Gunner" (p. 1166; SE p. 707)
Levertov, "Tenebrae" (p. 1249; SE p. 762): Compare Miles, "Mem-
    orial Day" (p. 1145; SE p. 699), another poem about the home
    front during the Vietnam War.
Henry Reed, "Lessons of the War" (p. 1171; SE p. 710)
Wilbur, "First Snow in Alsace" (p. 1218; SE p. 744)
Hecht, "'More Light! More Light!'" (p. 1236; SE p. 754): Compare
    Hecht's "The Feast of Stephen" (p. 1238; SE p. 756): what
    does it suggest about the impulses behind the atrocities de-
    scribed in "'More Light! More Light!'"?

7.5 Work

In teaching an introductory class in poetry it is sometimes hard to
avoid leaving students with the impression that poetry is concerned entirely with matters of leisure hours—love, art, mourning,
meditative walks, and moments of contemplation—and not with
the daily, tiring, unremarkable time spent working for a living.
Such an impression tends to suggest that poetry, too, is a luxury,
the result of idle hours, to be read in idle hours or in English
classes. Insofar as some of the poems listed below suggest that the
various kinds of work they describe may also be figures for the
poet's labors, they may help to open discussion about what kinds of
work the reading and writing of poetry is, as well as what kinds of
work it may treat. See also Section 7.9, Technology and Modern
Life.

Frost, "Mending Wall" (p. 908; SE p. 539) and "The Wood-Pile"
    (p. 912; SE p. 540)
Williams, "The Red Wheelbarrow" (p. 945; SE p. 561)
Lewis, "Sheepdog Trials in Hyde Park" (p. 1082; SE p. 658)
Bishop, "At the Fishhouses" (p. 1138; SE p. 693); and "Filling
    Station" (p. 1139; SE p. 695)
Miles, "Student" (p. 1144; SE p. 699)
Page, "The Stenographers" (p. 1203; SE p. 735)
Ammons, "Silver" (p. 1254; SE p. 764)

7.6 The Academy

Wallace Stevens said that "poetry is the scholar's art," but a
number of the poems in this group resist the bookishness and
academicism of the poetic enterprise in a number of ways (Yeats,
Cummings, Snodgrass); in doing so they may draw on a range of
erudite knowledge (Jarrell).

Yeats, "The Scholars" (p. 881; SE p. 518)
Cummings, "O sweet spontaneous" (p. 1040; SE p. 628) and "since
    feeling is first" (p. 1042; SE p. 629)
Miles, "Student (p. 1144) and "Memorial Day" (p. 1145; SE
    p. 699)
Jarrell, "Girl in a Library" (p. 1166; SE p. 707)
Snodgrass, "April Inventory" (p. 1287; SE p. 783)

7.7 Home and Family Life

It is a little surprising to realize how few poems are explicitly set
indoors or talk about the domestic part of what Jarrell in "Well
Water" calls "the dailiness of life." A house can be the site of
hospitality and shelter (Jonson, Bradstreet), or an entrapment or
illusion, a reminder of loss (Robinson, Bishop, Rich). See also the
sections on Children and Childhood (7.24) and on Marriage
(7.15.E).

Jonson, "Inviting a Friend to Supper" (p. 226; SE p. 116)
Bradstreet, "Here Follow Some Verses upon the Burning of Our
    House July 10th, 1666" (p. 325; SE p. 170): What aspects of
    domestic comfort does Bradstreet have to dismiss before she
    can fully feel that the destruction of her house responds to her
    "desire" (line 6) and is a blessing?
Coleridge, "Frost at Midnight" (p. 566; SE p. 297)
Robinson, "Eros Turannos" (p. 901; SE p. 534): Compare to
    Tennyson's "Mariana" (p. 698; SE p. 396) for another poem in
    which a woman is entrapped in a house by love.
Williams, "Danse Russe" (p. 944; SE p. 560): Compare to "Frost at
    Midnight," where again a father is awake in the house while
    his family sleeps.
Bishop, "Sestina" (p. 1142; SE p. 697)
Jarrell, "Well Water" (p. 1171; SE p. 710): Compare Hayden's
    "Those Winter Sundays" (p. 1158; SE p. 701).
Brooks, "kitchenette building" (p. 1182; SE p. 719)
Lowell, "My Last Afternoon with Uncle Devereux Winslow"
    (p. 1191; SE p. 725) and "The Withdrawal" (p. 1202; SE
    p. 733)
Koch, "You Were Wearing" (p. 1251; SE p. 763)
Rich, "Living in Sin" (p. 1309; SE p. 797) and "Toward the
    Solstice" (p. 1318; SE p. 801): Compare to Bradstreet, Brooks,

and Bishop: do the women poets on this list seem to have a more detailed sense than the men do of the "loving humdrum acts / of attention" ("Solstice," lines 99-100) that make up daily household life?

Heaney, "Sunlight" (p. 1383; SE p. 840)

7.8 The City

Poems of the city can reflect on the way the individual fates of the anonymous masses that populate the city are interwoven (Swift, Blake, Whitman, MacNeice, "Bagpipe Music"), or on the utter isolation of the individual when surrounded by the dense populace of the city (Eliot, Rich). You might wish to teach as a group the poems set in New York City, perhaps comparing them to the poems set in London.

Swift, "A Description of the Morning" (p. 392; SE p. 206) and "A Description of a City Shower" (p. 392; SE p. 206): How do morning and rain bring out the city's capacity for masking chaos? Why does "City Shower" begin with an orderly prediction of the weather from various signs, but end with an undifferentiated flood?

Pope, "Epistle of Miss Blount" (p. 423; SE p. 226): Is the city Miss Blount is reluctant to leave recognizably like the one in Swift's poems?

Blake, "London" (p. 506; SE p. 265): How and why are the civic institutions of the church, war, marriage, and prostitution interdependent? How can the "manacles" that these social institutions use to shackle the populace be "mind-forg'd"?

Wordsworth, "Composed Upon Westminster Bridge, September 3, 1802" (p. 550; SE p. 285): What makes this view of the city as beautiful as a country landscape? What will happen to this effect when the sun rises over the still, "smokeless" city?

Whitman, "Crossing Brooklyn Ferry" (p. 764; SE p. 442): Not about the city, but the sort of meditation possible only in crowds. Compare the multiplicity of people and sights Whitman lists to the hodepodge of Swift's city.

Sandburg, "Chicago" (p. 925; SE p. 548)

Pound, "In a Station of the Metro" (p. 963; SE p. 575): Compare to Wordsworth, "Westminster Bridge," where the city is compared to a pastoral or rural site or landscape.

Eliot, "Preludes" (p. 997; SE p. 597): Compare "Preludes" to O'Hara, "How to Get There" (p. 1286; SE p. 116) for its vision of the city as a collection of lonely rooms. "The Waste Land" (p. 1000; SE p. 599) could also be taught with this group.

Crane, "Proem: To Brooklyn Bridge" (p. 1058; SE p. 643)

Hughes, "Theme for English B" (p. 1069; SE p. 648)

Auden, "As I Walked Out One Evening" (p. 1099; SE p. 667): Compare this ballad for the modern city to some of the popular ballads.

MacNeice, "Bagpipe Music" (p. 1113; SE p. 676): Compare to O'Hara's vision of New York City as a blitz of signs, brand names, and random pleasures in "The Day Lady Died"; "London Rain" (p. 1114; SE p. 677).

Brooks, "kitchennette building" (p. 1182; SE p. 719)

Hugo, "Degrees of Gray in Philipsburg" (p. 1242; SE p. 757): As in the Levertov poem, Hugo connects a town with a memory of a particular time in his life.

Levertov, "From the Roof" (p. 1247; SE p. 761)

O'Hara "The Day Lady Died" (p. 1285; SE p. 781); "How to Get There" (p. 1286; SE p. 782)

Ginsberg, "In the Baggage Room at Greyhound" (p. 1278; SE p. 776)

Rich, "Living in Sin" (p. 1309; SE p. 797)

7.9 Technology and Modern Life

What unites this diverse group of poems is that they all include, as a central concern or just in passing, conveniences and conveyances of the industrial age: trains, cars, movies, photographs, suspension bridges, gas stations. It is useful to remind students that poetry can accommodate such things and the words that go along with them: poetic language can include "pickups and big semi's" (Stafford), "connecting rods" (Whitman), "elevators" (Crane), "on-coming traffic" (Roethke), even brand names and trademarks ("The Victor Dog," "Gauloises" [O'Hara], "Esso" [Bishop]); see also the sections on Diction (5.5.A and B). A number of the twentieth-century poems on The City (7.8) could be added to this group.

Whitman, "To a Locomotive in Winter" (p. 781; SE p. 456)

Williams, "The Young Housewife" (p. 944; SE p. 560)

Crane, from *The Bridge*, "Proem: To Brooklyn Bridge" (p. 1058; SE p. 643)

Roethke, "The Far Field" (p. 1121; SE p. 681)

Bishop, "Filling Station" (p. 1139; SE p. 695)

Miles, "Midweek" (p. 1143; SE p. 698); "Reason" (p. 1144; SE p. 698)

Stafford, "Traveling through the Dark" (p. 1174; SE p. 712); "Accountability" (p. 1175; SE p. 713)

Lowell, "Skunk Hour" (p. 1195; SE p. 728) and "Epilogue" (p. 1203; SE p. 735)

Page, "The Stenographers" (p. 1203; SE p. 735)

Bukowski, "vegas" (p. 1212; SE p. 740)

Merrill, "The Victor Dog" (p. 1282; SE p. 780)

O'Hara, "The Day Lady Died" (p. 1285; SE p. 781)

Ashbery, "Melodic Trains" (p. 1291; SE p. 785)
Gunn, "On the Move" (p. 1301; SE p. 792)
Walcott, "The Gulf" (p. 1333; SE p. 812)
Baraka, "In Memory of Radio" (p. 1356; SE p. 826)
Atwood, "This Is a Photograph of Me" (p. 1373; SE p. 836)

7.10 Nature

A very large number of poems could fit under this capacious rubric,
including those in sections 7.11, 7.12, 7.13, 7.14, and 7.20. The
poems selected for this group suggest in various ways that nature is
less the nonhuman world "out there" and more an index or mirror
of moral or spiritual qualities. Some of these poems outline how
topography shapes the ambitions, visions, and temper of the
creatures who inhabit it (Auden, Purdy). In others nature is chiefly
seen as a force of change; as such it may be inexorably rapacious
(Frost's "Design," Thomas, Everson), or gently balancing loss with
gain, so that "permanence / and transience fuse in a single body"
(Ammons, "The Put-Down Come On") and it creatures "use death
to remain alive" (Purdy, "Trees at the Arctic Circle").

Marvell, "The Garden" (p. 343; SE p. 182): The garden into which
  the poet retreats from human toil and ambition might seem
  itself to be rather laboriously and skillfully designed and culti-
  vated: is this a contradiction that needs to be resolved? Compare Swinburne's "A Forsaken Garden" (p. 842; SE p. 493).
Wordsworth, "I Wandered Lonely as a Cloud" (p. 556; SE p. 290):
  In which of the other poems on this list does nature seem to
  be chiefly something remembered or envisioned in the
  "inward eye"?
Whitman, from "Song of Myself," 6 ("A child said *What is the
  grass?* fetching it to me with full hands") (p. 760; SE p. 438)
Hopkins, "God's Grandeur" (p. 855; SE p. 502) and "Pied Beauty"
  (p. 855; SE p. 503)
Frost "Design" (p. 921; SE p. 545), "Come In," and "The Most of
  It" (pp. 922-23; SE p. 546)
Jeffers, "Carmel Point" (p. 984; SE p. 589): Compare Kavanagh's
  "Spraying the Potatoes" (p. 1088; SE p. 660): does Kavanagh
  see man as a "spoiler"? Both poems might be studied along
  with Burns's "To a Mouse" (p. 511; SE p. 268), where again to
  cultivate the land is to risk despoiling it in some way.
Auden, "In Praise of Limestone" (p. 1104; SE p. 670)
Kavanagh, "Shancoduff" (p. 1088; SE p. 660): In calling his hills
  "incurious" and "happy," or simply in labeling them "his,"
  does Kavanagh overstep the bounds of description and become
  "carried away" in Purdy's sense ("Trees at the Arctic
  Circle," line 43)?

Everson, "In All These Acts" (p. 1147; SE p. 700)
Thomas, "The Force That Through the Green Fuse Drives the
    Flower" (p. 1176; SE p. 713)
Lowell, "The Withdrawal" (p. 1202; SE p. 733)
Purdy, "Trees at the Arctic Circle" (p. 1206; SE p. 737)
Ammons, "Corsons Inlet" (p. 1255; SE p. 765); "The Put-Down
    Come On" (p. 1259; SE p. 768)

7.11 Flowers and Trees

Flowers are traditional emblems of the transience of beauty, and
hence useful cautionary tokens in seduction poems (Waller,
Herrick's "To Daffodils") or in meditations on mutability (Frost's
"Design"). But flowers and trees may just as readily be figures of
miraculous renewal or resilience (Herbert, Roethke, Hayden,
Purdy). Or their very uselessness can win the poet's admiration
(Emerson, Crane).

Waller, "Song" ("Go, lovely rose!") (p. 274; SE p. 146)
Herrick, "The Lily in a Crystal" (p. 245; SE 128); "To Daffodils"
    (p. 247; SE p. 130)
Herbert, "The Flower" (p. 264; SE p. 140)
Blake, "The Sick Rose" (p. 505; SE p. 263)
Emerson, "The Rhodora" (p. 666; SE p. 375)
Thoreau, "I Am a Parcel of Vain Strivings Tied" (p. 752; SE p. 434)
D. G. Rossetti, "The Woodspurge" (p. 798; SE p. 467)
Frost "Birches" (p. 914; SE p. 541); "Design" (p. 921; SE p. 545)
Lawrence, "Andraitx—Pomegranate Flowers" (p. 956; SE p. 568);
    "Bavarian Gentians" (p. 956; SE p. 568): Compare to H. D.'s
    "Sea Violet," where again a flower is seen as a source of light.
H. D., "Sea Violet" (p. 979; SE p. 585)
Crane, "Royal Palm" (p. 1059; SE p. 644)
Roethke, "Root Cellar" (p. 1117; SE p. 679)
Hayden, "The Night-Blooming Cereus" (p. 1159; SE p. 701)
Purdy, "Trees at the Arctic Circle" (p. 1206; SE p. 737)
Plath, "Elm" (p. 1351; SE p. 821)

7.12 Animals

Writing about animals may challenge poets' powers of description
and specificity, and test their abilities to describe non-human
creatures on their own terms. You might ask students to consider
the degree to which these poems turn animals into people: when a
poem carefully delineates and characterizes an animal, does it
necessarily tend to treat the animal as though it were human?
What kind of knowledge about animals can poets provide that
zoology cannot?

The tendency of animal poems to shift toward their end into moral reflections, in the manner of Aesop's fables, makes them useful for teaching poetic closure. How may writing about animals free poets from some of the constraints of decorum? What liberties of language may poets wish to take in order to capture these creatures so like and yet so unlike ourselves? What verbal stunts must poets try in order to keep up with these creatures' "spasmodic tricks of radiance" (Plath)?

Lovelace, "The Grasshopper" (p. 334; SE p. 176): How does Lovelace keep this from being the Aesopian prodigal grasshopper (the one who wouldn't listen to the frugal ant)?

Taylor, "Upon a Spider Catching a Fly" (p. 384; SE p. 199): From the minutely observed details of the first five stanzas, could we have predicted the turn to the moral lesson of the last five? What is the effect of the closing shift in man-animal comparisons from man as wasp caught in the devil's net to man as nightingale?

Gray, "Ode: On the Death of a Favorite Cat, Drowned in a Tub of Goldfishes" (p. 462; SE p. 247): Compare Gray's flip moral to Taylor's more studied one. To what degree is the difference dependent on the way Taylor compares human beings to animals, while Gray turns his animals into human beings? Compare both poems with others in this group that stress the savagery of animals, by Blake, Burns, Clare, Melville.

Smart, from "Jubilate Agno," lines 697-780 ("For I will consider my Cat Jeoffrey") (p. 470; SE p. 253): How does Smart manage so exact an inventory of "complete cat" (line 744), while all the time interpreting the cat's activities as worshipful, and in that sense as human and not cat-like? What is the effect of devoting a complete line to each action of the cat? Is there a narrative or some other principle of order to the sequence of activities Smart describes? This is a good text to focus on the language of animal poems. Smart's cat "camels his back" (line 755): what other unusual verbs does Smart introduce? A class exercise could emerge from this question: point out that names of some animals are conventionally used also as verbs (dog, fox, badger), and ask students to invent new idioms on the model of these or Smart's: what would it mean to "cat"? to "lamb"? to "spider"?

Cowper, "Epitaph on a Hare" (p. 481; SE p. 256): Compare to Gray's "Ode: On the Death of a Favorite Cat"; see section on Elegies.

Blake, "The Lamb" (p. 498; SE p. 260) and "The Tyger" (p. 505; SE p. 264): As line 17 of "The Lamb" tells us, this poem is spoken by a child. For this child, is the lamb a real, living creature, or a religious emblem? Who speaks in "The Tyger"? Line 20 asks what is probably the best question for thinking about the two poems together.

Clare, "Badger" (p. 641; SE p. 357): What accounts for the dispassionate tone in which this violent encounter is set forth? How does Clare shape our feelings about the savagery of the badger and of the men who hunt him? Why do men enjoy the badger's savagery as a display or sport? What happens when a creature from the wild is brought into the town?

Melville, "The Maldive Shark" (p. 759; SE p. 437): Is this a pilot-fish's-eye view of the shark? If this were an Aesop's fable, what would the moral be? Why doesn't Melville draw a moral? or does he?

Whitman, "A Noiseless Patient Spider" (p. 780; SE p. 456): Compare to Taylor, "Upon a Spider Catching a Fly": in each poem, what is signified by the spider's ability to spin his web out of himself? Compare to Shelley, "To a Skylark" (p. 624; SE p. 357): how do Whitman and Shelley make an animal into a figure for their own poetic aspirations? A class exercise: complete Tennyson, "The Eagle" (p. 713; SE p. 410) and Melville, "The Maldive Shark" with a Whitmanian ending, a comparison between the animal and the poet, perhaps starting with "And you, O my soul . . ." In which case are the results a parody of Whitman?

Dickinson, Poem 986 ("A narrow Fellow in the Grass") (p. 814; SE p. 477): This poem is like a riddle; the answer is "a snake". Students will have other guesses, though, and it can be useful to list the clues that allow us to zero in on the identification of this ordinary and yet mysterious creature. Why does Dickinson, like Shelley in "To a Skylark" (p. 357), describe the snake largely in terms of things that are like it? Why is this snake frightening? Can a poet write about a snake without invoking the story of the serpent in the Garden of Eden?

Williams, "Poem" (p. 946; SE p. 562): Compare Williams's short, enjambed lines and Smart's long, end-stopped ones as two methods of representing the way cats move. Williams's title suggests that his version is also about the way poems move.

Lawrence, "Snake" (p. 952; SE p. 566): Compare to Dickinson's "A narrow Fellow in the Grass." Lawrence's poem might also be studied in the context of a number of poems centering on an unexpected encounter between a person and an animal, including Frost's "The Most of It" (p. 923; SE p. 546) and the selections listed below by Bishop ("The Armadillo"), Lowell ("Skunk Hour"), Nemerov, and Wright.

Moore, "Peter" (p. 989; SE p. 591)

Muir, "The Animals" (p. 991; SE p. 592)

Birney, "The Bear on the Delhi Road" (p. 1079; SE p. 656)

Lewis, "Sheepdog Trials in Hyde Park" (p. 1082; SE p. 658)

Warren, "Sila" (p. 1091; SE p. 662)

Bishop, "The Fish" (p. 1136; SE p. 692) and "The Armadillo" (p. 1141; SE p. 696)

Lowell, "Mr. Edwards and the Spider" (p. 1188; SE p. 724) and "Skunk Hour" (p. 1195; SE p. 728)

Nemerov, "The Goose Fish" (p. 1215; SE p. 742): What is the function of the closing mention of the zodiac, with its constellations representing animals (including Pisces, the fish)?

Wilbur, "The Death of a Toad" (p. 1221; SE p. 746)

Larkin, "Myxomatosis" (p. 1229; SE p. 750)

Ammons, "Silver" (p. 1254; SE p. 764)

Wright, "Discoveries in Arizona" (p. 1300; SE p. 791)

Hughes, "The Thought-Fox" (p. 1323; SE p. 806); "The Bull Moses" (p. 1324; SE p. 807); "A March Calf" (p. 1327; SE p. 807)

Atwood, "The Animals in That Country" (p. 1374; SE p. 836)

7.13 Birds

In their capacity to sing and to soar, birds often figure as some version of poets, and poems about birds tend to be meditations on the art of poetry itself. Why do these poetic birds tend to grow less melodious in the twentieth century?

Sidney, "The Nightingale" (p. 154; SE p. 79)

Shelley, "To a Skylark" (p. 624; SE p. 357): Compare the advantages over mankind that Shelley attributes to the skylark with those that Burns attributes to his creature in "To a Mouse." How does Shelley's series of likenesses for the skylark depend on the poet's not being able to see it, but only to hear its song? Which other poems in this list or in the one on Animal delineate an animal by asking it, at least implicitly, "What is most like thee"?

Keats, "Ode to a Nightingale" (p. 660; SE p. 370)

Tennyson, "The Eagle" (p. 713; SE p. 410): Although the poem gives the eagle "hands" and enables him to "stand," this bird does not seem to be turned into a person. Why not?

Dickinson, Poem 328 ("A Bird came down the Walk") (p. 808; SE p. 474) and Poem 1463 ("A Route of Evanescence") (p. 816; SE p. 478): In the first poem, what kinds of observations does Dickinson make when the bird is unaware of her? How does her knowledge—and her language—about the bird change when it becomes aware of her presence? How close does the speaker get to the bird in other poems in this group, and with what differences in effect? Sending "A Route of Evanescence" to a friend, Dickinson wrote, "Please accept a Humming Bird." Your students may suggest other possible answers to this riddle. What characteristics of hummingbirds make this cryptic poem suited to them?

Hardy, "The Darkling Thrush" (p. 846; SE p. 497): On the eve of the twentieth century, the poet hears a diminished version of those lush birdsongs of the English literary tradition. Hardy's original title for this poem was "By the Century's Death-Bed." Does the poem end on a note of hope or gloom? Compare the bleak landscape against which this thrush sings to the landscape in which Keats's nightingale sings.

Hopkins, "The Windhover" (p. 855; SE p. 503)

Frost, "The Oven Bird" (p. 914; SE p. 541)

Thomas, "The Owl" (p. 926; SE p. 549)

Stevens, "Thirteen Ways of Looking at a Blackbird" (p. 932; SE p. 555)

Jeffers, "Hurt Hawks" (p. 983; SE p. 588)

Plath, "Black Rook in Rainy Weather" (p. 1345; SE p. 818): This poem might be studied with a number of others in which someone encounters a natural creature and speculates on what it signifies, such as Emerson's "The Rhodora" (p. 666; SE p. 375), Stafford's "Traveling through the Dark" (p. 1174; SE p. 712), and Nemerov's "The Goose Fish" (p. 1215; SE p. 742)

7.14 Bodies of Water

A. Sea and Seashore

The poems on this list figure sea and seashore in a variety of ways: the sea as a dynamic realm of constant destruction (Cowper, Hardy, Williams); as a force for preservation and transformation (Shakespeare); or as a mysterious, murky realm that counters, underlies, or mirrors our own solid earthly existence (Poe, Millay). How do figurations of the sea and shore change over history? The present-day sense that the seashore is a natural place for meditative walks and romantic meetings (the popularity of this topos is evident from its commercial version in soft-focus photos on greeting cards of couples wandering on beaches in a sunset glow) seems not to emerge strongly in poetry until the nineteenth century (Whitman, Arnold, Stevens).

Spenser, "Amoretti," 75 ("One day I wrote her name upon the strand") (p. 137; SE p. 67)

Shakespeare, "Full Fathom Five" (p. 197; SE p. 94): Is the sea deadly or purifying? Do other poems on this list concern a "sea change" of some sort?

Cowper, "The Castaway" (p. 485; SE p. 257)

Poe, "The City in the Sea" (p. 695; SE p. 394)

Tennyson, "Crossing the Bar" (p. 716; SE p. 412)

Whitman, "Out of the Cradle Endlessly Rocking" (p. 770; SE p. 446): Why does the child's initiation into some sort of poetic calling take place at the seashore? Compare Whitman's treatment of the seashore in "Song of Myself," Section 11

("Twenty-eight young men bathe by the shore") (p. 761; SE p. 439).

Arnold, "Dover Beach" (p. 794; SE p. 463): Compare Arnold's treatment of the sea in "To Marguerite" (p. 783; SE p. 457).

Hardy, "The Convergence of the Twain" (p. 848; SE p. 499): Compare to the awful stillness of underwater worlds in Shakespeare, "Full Fathom Five" and Poe, "The City in the Sea."

Stevens, "The Idea of Order at Key West" (p. 934; SE p. 556)

Williams, "The Yachts" (p. 947; SE p. 502)

Eliot, from *Four Quartets*, "The Dry Salvages" (p. 1013; SE p. 611)

Millay, "Above These Cares" (p. 1034; SE p. 624)

Hugo, "Salt Water Story" (p. 1244; SE p. 759)

Rich, "Diving into the Wreck" (p. 1315; SE p. 798): Compare Millay, "Above These Cares": what sort of mental or spiritual condition does the undersea world represent in each poem?

B. Water and Reflection

"Meditation and water are wedded forever, " Melville wrote of people gazing out to sea; but it seems that a still body of standing water, a mirror-like surface that holds reflections, most often figures mental reflection.

Traherne, "Shadows in the Water" (p. 379; SE p. 196)

Frost, "Spring Pools" (p. 919; SE p. 543)

Hollander, "Swan and Shadow" (p. 1308; SE p. 796)

7.15 Love

Like nature, romantic love is a topic that never goes out of fashion in poetry, and any number of possible groupings of poems could make a good lesson in reading love poetry. The general list below illustrates the range of tones and approaches to the subject; the more specific lists that follow gather poems centering on seduction, fidelity and infidelity, farewells and absences, sex, and marriage. See also the section on Love Sonnets (3.1.B).

Chaucer, "To Rosamond" (p. 49; SE p. 19) and "Merciless Beauty" (p. 51; SE p. 21)

D'Orléans, "The Smiling Mouth" (p. 52; SE p. 22)

Anonymous, "Western Wind" (p. 61; SE p. 29)

Anonymous, "There Is a Lady Sweet and Kind" (p. 88; SE p. 48)

Wyatt, "The Long Love That in My Thought Doth Harbor" (p. 89; SE p. 49)

Surrey, "Love, That Doth Reign and Live Within My Thought" (p. 98; SE p. 54)

Sidney, "Ring Out Your Bells" (p. 155; SE p. 79)
Wotton, "On His Mistress, the Queen of Bohemia" (p. 203; SE
    p. 99): Compare to other poems in this group that praise the
    beloved (Byron, Cummings, Roethke).
Donne, "The Good-Morrow" (p. 204; SE p. 100)
Jonson, "Though I Am Young and Cannot Tell" (p. 238; SE p. 122)
Herbert, "Love (III)" (p. 268; SE p. 141)
Marvell, "The Definition of Love" (p. 340; SE p. 181)
Blake, "The Garden of Love" (p. 506; SE p. 265)
Byron, "She walks in Beauty" (p. 589; SE p. 318)
Williams, "The Ivy Crown" (p. 950; SE p. 564)
Cummings, "somewhere i have never travelled, gladly beyond"
    (p. 1043; SE p. 630): Could this poem conceivably be spoken
    by a man or a woman, to a man or a woman?
Roethke, "I Knew a Woman" (p. 1120; SE p. 680)
Snyder, "Four Poems for Robin" (p. 1330; SE p. 810)
Ondaatje, "Gold and Black" (p. 1388; SE p. 844)

A. Seduction

The coy lady of Renaissance lyric called upon all the inventive
allurements of the passionate lover. Most of the poems on this list
employ some version of the *carpe diem* motif, advising the woman
to "seize the day" and yield to her suitor before her youth and
charms fade and she is no longer desirable. Questions of love and
mortality are thus curiously intertwined in a number of poems in
the Renaissance tradition of seduction lyrics.

How can we reconcile the picture of women as unyielding and
in need of elaborate persuasions to love presented in these pooems
with the frequent suggestion in poems in the next group (Fidelity
and Infidelity) that women are loose and faithless? On the model
of Ralegh's parodic "reply" to Marlowe's shepherd, or of Parker's
"One Perfect Rose," you might have students frame the woman's
response to some of the poems in this list.

Elizabeth I, "When I Was Fair and Young" (p. 100; SE p. 55): What
    is the price of being a coy mistress, according to this poem?
Marlowe, "The Passionate Shepherd to His Love" (p. 185; SE
    p. 87): The effectiveness of the shepherd's ploys may be
    judged by reading along with this poem Ralegh's "The
    Nymph's Reply to the Shepherd" (p. 105; SE p. 87) and
    Lewis's modern rendition, "Song" ("Come, live with me and
    be my love") (p. 1081; SE po. 657)
Shakespeare, "Oh Mistress Mine" (p. 195; SE p. 93)
Campion, "My Sweetest Lesbia" (p. 198; SE p. 95)
Jonson, "Come, My Celia" (p. 237; SE p. 121)
Herrick, "Corinna"s Going A-Maying" (p. 244; SE p. 127); "To the
    Virgins, to Make Much of Time" (p. 246; SE p. 129)

Waller, "Song" ("Go, lovely rose!") (p. 274; SE p. 146)
Marvell, "To His Coy Mistress" (p. 337; SE p. 178)
Goldsmith, "When Lovely Woman Stoops to Folly" (p. 472; SE p. 255): A useful reminder that if the woman *does* seize the day, she may be subject to social censure, as the man is not.
Parker, "One Perfect Rose" (p. 1038; SE p. 627)
Cummings, "since feeling is first" (p. 1042; SE p. 629): What devices of Renaissance seduction poems does Cummings rework? What is the effect of the Renaissance flavor of the vow "lady i swear by all flowers"?

B. Fidelity and Infidelity

Anonymous, (Popular Ballads), "The Unquiet Grave" (p. 75; SE p. 39) and "Bonny Barbara Allan" (p. 77; SE p. 41)
Anonymous, "As You Came from the Holy Land of Walsingham" (p. 85; SE p. 46)
Wyatt, "They Flee from Me" (p. 91; SE p. 50)
Shakespeare, Sonnet 116 ("Let me not to the marriage of true minds" (p. 190; SE p. 90)
Donne, "Woman's Constancy" (p. 206; SE p. 101), "The Anniversary" (p. 209; SE p. 104), "The Funeral" (p. 214; SE p. 108), and "The Relic" (p. 215; SE p. 108)
Carew, "Song. To My Inconstant Mistress" (p. 270; SE p. 144)
Suckling, "Song" (p. 317; SE p. 166)
Burns, "John Anderson, My Jo" (p. 517; SE p. 272), "Bonnie Doon" (p. 521; SE p. 272), and "A Red, Red Rose" (p. 522; SE p. 273)
Byron, "When We Two Parted" (p. 589; SE p. 319)
Keats, "La Belle Dame sans Merci" (p. 658; SE p. 368)
Raab, "Attack of the Crab Monsters" (p. 1399; SE p. 851)

C. Farewells and Absences

Drayton, from "Idea," 61 ("Since there"s no help, come let us kiss and part") (p. 170; SE p. 87)
Donne, "Song" ("Sweetest love, I do not go") (p. 203; SE p. 103), "A Valediction: Of Weeping" (p. 210; SE p. 105), and "A Valediction: Forbidding Mourning" (p. 212; SE p. 105)
Bradstreet, "A Letter to Her Husband, Absent upon Public Employment" (p. 324; SE p. 170)
Lovelace, "To Lucasta, Going to the Wars" (p. 333; SE p. 176)
Byron, "So We'll Go No More A-Roving" (p. 592; SE p. 312)
Brontë, "Remembrance" (p. 754; SE p. 435)
Merwin, "Separation" (p. 1296; SE p. 790)

D. Sex

The topic of sex is not entirely divorced from the topic of Love, of course, and some of the poems in one list might with equal pertinence be listed in the other. Asking students to categorize some of these poems under either topic might lead to provocative discussions. Which poems in this list argue that sex is not a natural component of love but its enemy, or an activity that may or may not have anything to do with love (Graves, Millay)? Most of these poems see sex from the man's point of view; do the women on this list write about sex differently from the way the men do?

Shakespeare, Sonnet 129 ("Th' expense of spirit in a waste of shame") (p. 190; SE p. 90)

Donne, "The Ecstasy" (p. 213; SE p. 106); "Elegy XIX. To His Mistress Going to Bed" (p. 216; SE p. 110)

Herrick, "The Vine" (p. 242; SE p. 126); "Upon Julia's Breasts" (p. 247; SE p. 130)

Blake, "The Garden of Love" (p. 506; SE p. 265); "A Question Answered" (p. 508; SE p. 266); "I Askéd a Thief" (p. 507; SE p. 265)

Byron, from *Don Juan* (p. 592; SE p. 321)

Keats, "The Eve of St. Agnes" (p. 650; SE p. 360): The sexual consummation—if it is such—occurs in stanza 36. But the force of Keatsian sensuality is perhaps most strongly felt in the stanzas on Madeline undressing (stanzas 23-27): the picture of Madeline unclasping her "warmed jewels one by one" is arguably more titillating than anything in the randy Elizabethans. (For a comparison with the brittle eroticism of a century earlier, glance at Belinda's dressing room in Pope, "The Rape of the Lock," Canto I, lines 121-148.)

Whitman, from "Song of Myself," Section 24: "Walt Whitman, a kosmos, of Manhattan the son" (p. 762; SE p. 440): perhaps compare with Williams, "Danse Russe" (p. 944; SE p. 560) for another kind of celebration of the poet's own body, though for Williams it is his separateness from others that inspires his private self-involved dance.

Dickinson, Poem 249 ("Wild Nights—Wild Nights!") (p. 806; SE p. 473)

Williams, "Queen-Ann's-Lace" (p. 945; SE p. 561): Compare to Shakespeare, Sonnet 130 ("My mistress' eyes are nothing like the sun") (p. 190; SE p. 90), where again the lover rejects conventional comparisons for the lady's beauty.

Millay, "I, Being Born a Woman and Distressed" (p. 1033; SE p. 624)

Graves, "Down, Wanton, Down!") (p. 1051; SE p. 636): The title alludes to the fool's bawdy lines in *King Lear* (II.iv.119ff.): "*Lear:* O me, my heart; my rising heart! But down! *Fool:* Cry to it, uncle, as the cockney did to the eels when she put 'em i' th' paste alive. She knapp'd 'em o' th' coxcombs with a stick, and cried 'Down, wantons, down!'" How does this allusion further the speaker's witty polemic against his brutish and undiscriminating sexual drives?

Hope, "The Elegy" (p. 1108; SE p. 672): Donne's "Elegy XIX" took us to the moment before sex, and Hope's elegy picks up the conversation after that moment. Could you mistake this for a seventeeth-century poem? What is modern about Hope's version?

Purdy, "Love at Roblin Lake" (p. 1205; SE p. 736)

Creeley, "A Wicker Basket" (p. 1269; SE p. 775)

Rich, "The Ninth Symphony of Beethoven Understood at Last as a Sexual Message" (p. 1317; SE p. 800)

Lorde, "Recreation" (p. 1363; SE p. 840)

Stallworthy, "The Source" (p. 1365; SE p. 831)

Heaney, from Glanmore Sonnets, 10 ("I dreamt we slept in a moss in Donegal") (p. 1386; SE p. 843)

Ondaatje, "Burning Hills" (P. 1389; SE p. 844)

E. Marriage

Spenser, "Epithalamion" (p. 138; SE p. 68)

Taylor, "Upon Wedlock, and Death of Children" (p. 383; SE p. 198)

Meredith, "Modern Love" (p.. 801; SE p. 469)

Robinson, "Eros Turannos" (p. 901; SE p. 534)

Rich, "Living in Sin" (p. 1309; SE p. 797)

Merrill, "Upon a Second Marriage" (p. 1280; SE p. 779)

Corso, "Marriage" (p. 1321; SE p. 804): Why is the self-pitying, whining voice of the speaker so appealing? Compare Corso's picture of marriage, as a social institution to which there is great pressure to conform, to Spenser's picture of it as a triumphal procession? Which poem is more candid about the sexual impulses that marriage legitimates?

7.16 Science

See also Section 7.9, Technology and Modern Life.

Poe, "Sonnet—To Science" (p. 694; SE p. 393)

Whitman, "When I Heard the Learn'd Astronomer" (p. 764; SE p. 441)

Dickinson, Poem 185 ("'Faith' is a fine invention") (p. 804; SE p. 472)

Millay, "Euclid Alone Has Looked on Beauty Bare" (p. 1033; SE p. 623): The poems in this group by Poe, Whitman, and Cummings seem to agree that science and imagination (beauty, nature) are incompatible: what rebuttal is suggested in Millay's view of geometry's exclusive access to beauty?

Cummings, "O sweet spontaneous" (p. 1040; SE p. 628)

A. Enumeration

Poems in which specific sums are counted or amounts are calcu-
lated present an interesting series of issues about the differences
between the kinds of claims poetry and science make. What could
be more prosaic than an arithmetical sum? Yet in "Loveliest of
Trees" Housman manages to subtract 20 from 70 and come up
with the right answer, and in section 11 of "Song of Myself"
Whitman specifies that he is concerned with exactly "Twenty-eight
young men." What is the effect of this numerical specificity, and
why is it something we generally do not expect from poems? Why
does a ballad about "The Three Ravens" seem to name the right
number for a poem to be able to count, but a poem called, say,
"The Thirty-three Ravens" might veer toward parody? (And yet
Yeats can count fifty-nine swans with no parodic intent.) Questions
of diction arise here as well, and you might compare the way
poems indicate large amounts of things or vast distances, and the
way science does (what could be a more poetic unit of measure-
ment than a "light year"?).

Anonymous, "Mary Hamilton" (p. 80; SE p. 42): The subtraction of
  one from four in the final stanza reveals a surprise; in light of
  this little arithmetic problem, is it merely coincidence that
  the poem (like most ballads) alternates lines of four and three
  beats?
Suckling, "Out Upon It!" (p. 322; SE p. 167): How is it characteristic of this speaker to think small numbers are something to
  make a fuss over ("three whole days") and big numbers something to be tossed off lightly ("a dozen dozen")?
Marvell, "To His Coy Mistress" (p. 337; SE p. 178): Note especially
  lines 13-16: how do these vast sums of years distributed for
  various tasks of praise help to further the lover's suit?
Housman, "Loveliest of Trees, the Cherry Now" (p. 861; SE p. 506)
Whitman, "Song of Myself," section 11 (p. 761; SE p. 439)
Yeats, "The Wild Swans at Coole" (p. 880; SE p. 516): How does
  the exact count of "nine-and-fifty swans" figure into the poet's
  summing of his own autumnal years? Note also the curious
  specificity of the "nine bean-rows" in Yeats's "The Lake Isle of
  Innisfree" (p. 876; SE p. 515).
Miles, "Midweek" (p. 1143; SE p. 698): Miles enables us to hear
  what English sounds like when it counts: why is a phrase like
  "nine seven two seven one," although rhythmic and "easy to
  remember," not the sort of language we expect or usually find
  in poems?
Reed, from *Lessons of the War*: "Judging Distances" (p. 1171; SE
  p. 711)

7.17 Social and Political Protest

What special resources does poetry have to register resentment against injustice, corruption, war and violence, national policy, or the general malaise of civilization? Can a poem include or imply a reasoned political argument, or must it be merely an impassioned outcry of rage?

Ralegh, "The Lie" (p. 107; SE p. 60)
Milton, "On the Late Massacre in Piedmont" (p. 293; SE p. 164)
Blake, "London" (p. 506; SE p. 265); from *Milton*, "And Did Those Feet" (p. 510; SE p. 266); and from *Jerusalem*, "England! Awake! Awake! Awake!" (p. 510; SE p. 267)
Wordsworth, "London, 1802" (p. 550; SE p. 285)
Shelley, "England in 1819" (p. 620; SE p. 337)
Hardy, "Channel Firing" (p. 849; SE p. 500): How does Hardy's poem give bite to the dull cliché that something (in this case the guns of war) is "loud enough to wake the dead"?
Yeats, "Easter 1916" (p. 881; SE p. 518)
Jeffers, "Shine, Perishing Republic" (p. 981; SE p. 588)
Cummings, "'next to of course god america i'" and "i sing of Olaf glad and big" (p. 1042; SE p. 629)
Eberhart, "The Fury of Aerial Bombardment" (p. 1085; SE p. 659): Compare Hardy's "Channel Firing" (p. 849; SE p. 500).
Warren, "Dream, Dump-heap, and Civilization" (p. 1094; SE p. 664): Compare Wilbur's "Junk" (p. 1224; SE p. 747). What is the relation between the three items listed in the title? What kinds of "complicity" does the poem suggest between the junkpile and the moments of violence recalled from childhood?
Miles, "Memorial Day" (p. 1145; SE p. 699)
Hecht, "'More Light! More Light!'" (p. 1236; SE p. 754)
Levertov, "Tenebrae" (p. 1249; SE p. 762)
Walcott, "The Gulf" (p. 1333; SE p. 812)

7.18 Art

I am taking "art" as broadly as possible: art may be painting (Browning, Ashbery), any medium through which reality appears more fascinating or more palatable (Herrick), or even a doily ornamenting a filthy gas station (Bishop).

Herrick, "The Lily in a Crystal" (p. 245; SE p. 128): How are Herrick's aesthetics in this poem like that in his "Delight in Disorder" (p. 243; SE p. 126)?
Browning, "Fra Lippo Lippi" (p. 723; SE p. 419) and "Andrea del Sarto" (p. 737; SE p. 428)
Yeats, "Lapis Lazuli" (p. 891; SE p. 527)

Auden, "Musée des Beaux Arts" (p. 1100; SE p. 668): Compare Williams's "The Dance," which also describes a painting by Brueghel.
Wilbur, "Museum Piece" (p. 1221; SE p. 745)
Ashbery, "The Painter" (p. 1289; SE p. 784)

A. Women and Art

It can be instructive to study poems that examine women as artists along with those that exalt women as works of art. The poems by Marvell, Poe, Browning, and Pound examine the relation between women and works of art, and specifically the tendency in men to turn women into works of art so that they may be more readily gazed at, controlled, and possessed.

Marvell, "The Gallery" (p. 338; SE p. 179): In this tour through the contradictory iconography of woman (as seen through men's eyes), note how often artistic or trans-shaping tendencies are attributed to women.
Poe, "To Helen" (p. 695; SE p. 394)
Browning, "My Last Duchess" (p. 717; SE p. 413): How is the Duke's view of art as a means of possessing women different from that of Browning's artists, "Fra Lippo Lippi" (p. 723; SE p. 419) and "Andrea del Sarto" (p. 737; SE p. 428)?
C. Rossetti, "In an Artist's Studio" (p. 818; SE p. 479)
Yeats, "Adam's Curse" (p. 879; SE p. 516)
Pound, "Portrait d'une Femme" (p. 959; SE p. 572)
Rich, "Aunt Jennifer's Tigers" (p. 1309; SE p. 796)

7.19 Music

Poems about music often reflect on the musical powers of verse. What powers are attributed to music? What distinctions are made between instrumental and vocal music? Why are most of the singers in these poems women?

Campion, "When to Her Lute Corinna Sings" (p. 199; SE p. 95)
Marvell, "The Fair Singer" (p. 340; SE p. 181)
Dryden, "A Song for St. Cecilia's Day" (p. 375; SE p. 193)
Wordsworth, "The Solitary Reaper" (p. 559; SE p. 292)
Shelley, "To Jane: The Keen Stars Were Twinkling" (p. 639; SE p. 354)
E. B. Browning, "A Musical Instrument" (p. 675; SE p. 381)
Browning, "A Toccata of Galuppi's" (p. 730; SE p. 426)
Lawrence, "Piano" (p. 952; SE p. 565)
Hughes, "The Weary Blues" (p. 1067; SE p. 647)

Merrill, "The Victor Dog" (p. 1282; SE p. 780): Is modern tech-
nology a substitute for the memory in which Wordsworth could
preserve a song after it was heard no more ("The Solitary
Reaper")?
Rich, "The Ninth Symphony of Beethoven Understood at Last as a
Sexual Message" (p. 1317; SE p. 800)

7.20 Seasons and Seasonal Change

Poems about seasonal change lend themselves to meditation on
mortality (Hopkins, Lowell), on the genuine necessities of life in
the face of the years' ravages (Lovelace), and on the mystery of
change in nature or in oneself (Dickinson, Rich).

Lovelace, "The Grasshopper" (p. 334; SE p. 176)
Dickinson, Poem 1540 ("As imperceptibly as Grief") (p. 816; SE
p. 478)
Hopkins, "Spring and Fall" (p. 857; SE p. 504)
Lowell, "The Withdrawal" (p. 1202; SE p. 733)
Rich, "Toward the Solstice" (p. 1318; SE p. 801)

A. Spring and Summer

Anonymous, "The Cuckoo Song" (p. 3; SE p. 3)
Surrey, "The Soote Season" (p. 97; SE p. 654): Compare to Carew's
"The Spring" and to Rossetti's "Barren Spring," in which
again the beloved is not as warm as the weather.
Shakespeare, "When Daisies Pied" (p. 193; SE p. 91) and "It Was a
Lover and His Lass" (p. 194; SE p. 92)
Nashe, "Spring, the Sweet Spring" (p. 201; SE p. 97)
Herrick, "Corinna's Going A-Maying" (p. 244; SE p. 127)
Carew, "The Spring" (p. 269; SE p. 143)
Browning, "Home-Thoughts, From Abroad" (p. 720; SE p. 416)
D. G. Rossetti, "Barren Spring" (p. 800; SE p. 468)
Eliot, "The Waste Land" (p. 1000; SE p. 599)
Lowell, "This Golden Summer" (p. 1201; SE p. 733)
Crase, "Summer" (p. 1395; SE p. 848): Compare to Dickinson's
Poem 1540 ("As imperceptibly as Grief") (p. 816; SE p. 478):
what small alterations register the arrival or departure of
summer in each poem? How do both Crase and Dickinson
suggest that the change of season is also an inner, spiritual
condition?

B. Fall and Winter

In some of these poems, winter's barrenness and sterility may spur
the imagination (Hecht) or may draw the human community closer

together (Campion, Shakespeare's "When icicles hang by the wall,"
Frost's "The Wood-pile," Stafford); in others it isolates the in-
dividual from the community, or seems a harbinger of death
(Dickinson, Frost's "Stopping by Woods on a Snowy Evening").
Winter may be as much a spiritual state—a "mind of winter," in the
words of Stevens's "The Snow Man"—as a state of nature (Hardy,
Wilbur), or a time of life as well as a time of year (Shakespeare's
Sonnet 73).

Shakespeare, Sonnet 73 ("That time of year thou mayst in me
    behold") (p. 189; SE p. 89); "When Daisies Pied" ("When
    icicles hang by the wall") (p. 193; SE p. 92); and "Blow, Blow,
    Thou Winter Wind" (p. 194; SE p. 92)
Campion, "Now Winter Nights Enlarge" (p. 200; SE p. 96)
Keats, "To Autumn" (p. 664; SE p. 373)
Meredith, "Winter Heavens" (p. 803; SE p. 471)
Dickinson, "There's a certain Slant of light" (p. 806; SE p. 474)
Hardy, "The Darkling Thrush" (p. 846; SE p. 497)
Stevens, "The Snow Man" (p. 928; SE p. 550)
Frost, "Stopping by Woods on a Snowy Evening" (p. 917; SE
    p. 542) and "The Wood-pile" (p. 912; SE p. 540)
Hayden, "Those Winter Sundays" (p. 1158; Se p. 701)
Stafford, "Accountability" (p. 1175; Se p. 713)
Wilbur, "Boy at the Window" (p. 1222; SE p. 746)
Hecht, "Sestina d'Inverno" (p. 1142; SE p. 755)
O'Hara, "How to Get There" (p. 1286; SE p. 782)

7.21 Happiness and Dejection

This section includes a range of varied poems dealing with states of
brief, ecstatic epiphanies, or of emotional crisis or psychic extrem-
ity. Most of the poems about dejection or joy will be love poems,
elegies, or religious or devotional poems. How do these poems
suggest that there are fashions or changing historical trends in joy
and happiness? Is what the Romantics call "dejection" the same
emotion we call "depression," or what Dickinson calls "a formal
feeling" (Poem 341)? Do tears, like maidenly blushes or fits of
swooning, go in and out of fashion as expressions of feeling? As
presented in these poems, which seems more an expression of
historical conventions of feeling: happiness or dejection?

A. Happiness

Milton, "L'Allegro" (p. 284; SE p. 156)
Blake, from *Songs of Innocence*, "Introduction" ("Piping down the
    valleys wild") (p. 497; SE p. 259)
Wordsworth, "I Wandered Lonely as a Cloud" (p. 556; SE p. 290)

Dickinson, Poem 214 ("I taste a liquor never brewed") (p. 804; SE
 p. 472)
Williams, "Danse Russe" (p. 944; SE p. 560)
Levertov, "From the Roof" (p. 1247; SE p. 761)
Bly, "Driving Toward the Lac Qui Parle River" (p. 1268; SE p. 775):
 Compare to Wright's "A Blessing," another poem in which the
 speaker arrives at a moment of extraordinary happiness on an
 ordinary road in Minnesota.
Wright, "A Blessing" (p. 1297; SE p. 791)

B. Dejection

Wyatt, "My Galley Charged with Forgetfulness" (p. 90; SE p. 50)
Donne, "A Valediction: Of Weeping" (p. 210; SE p. 105)
Herbert, "Affliction (I)" (p. 255; SE p. 134) and "The Flower"
 (p. 264; SE p. 140)
Milton, "Il Penseroso" (p. 287; SE p. 159)
Coleridge, "Dejection: An Ode" (p. 581; SE p. 312)
Shelley, "Stanzas Written in Dejection, Near Naples" (p. 619; SE
 p. 336)
Keats, "Ode on Melancholy" (p. 662; SE p. 371)
D. G. Rossetti, "The Woodspurge" (p. 798; SE p. 467)
Dickinson, Poem 280 ("I felt a Funeral, in my Brain") (p. 806; SE
 p. 474) and Poem 341 ("After great pain, a formal feeling
 comes") (p. 808; SE p. 476)
Hardy, "In Tenebris" (p. 847; SE p. 498)
Hughes, "The Weary Blues" (p. 1067; SE p. 647)
Roethke, "In a Dark Time" (p. 1123; SE p. 683)
Berryman, from "The Dream Songs," 29 ("There sat down, once a
 thing on Henry's heart") (p. 1163; SE p. 705)
Lowell, "Skunk Hour" (p. 1195; SE p. 728)

7.22 Religion

See also the sections on Devotional or Religious Sonnets (3.1.C)
and on Biblical Stories (8.4).

Anonymous, "The Bitter Withy" (p. 83; SE p. 45)
Donne, "Holy Sonnets" (p. 220; SE p. 112)
Jonson, "A Hymn to God the Father" (p. 231; SE p. 120)
Crashaw, "A Hymn to the Name and Honor of the Admirable Saint
 Teresa" (p. 327; SE p. 172)
Frost, "Directive" (p. 924; SE p. 547)
Larkin, "Church Going" (p. 1227; SE p. 749)
Merrill, "Whitebeard on Videotape" (p. 1283; SE p. 781): A
 reminder that the topic of religion is not just about Christian

religion, but has to do with the need to have something to believe in or— in Merrill's poem— a quick "detergent" to cleanse "everyone's dirty linen."

A. Omnipresence of God

Hopkins, "Pied Beauty" (p. 855; SE p. 503): Compare Ammons's "The City Limits" (p. 1252; SE p. 769): is Ammons's a religious poem?
Everson, "In All These Acts" (p. 1147; SE p. 700)

B. Faith and Doubt

Herbert, "Affliction (I)" (p. 255; SE p. 134) and "The Collar (p. 262; SE p. 138)
Milton, "When I Consider How My Light Is Spent" (p. 293; SE p. 164)
Dickinson, Poem 185 ("'Faith' is a fine invention") (p. 804; SE p. 472)

C. Prayers and Entreaties

Nashe, "A Litany in Time of Plague" (p. 202; SE p. 98)
Donne, "Hymn to God My God, in My Sickness" (p. 223; SE p. 113)
Jonson, "A Hymn to God the Father" (p. 231; SE p. 120)
Herbert, "Prayer (I)" (p. 256; SE p. 135)
Pope, "The Universal Prayer" (p. 430; SE p. 227)
Dickinson, Poem 49 ("I never lost as much but twice") (p. 804; SE p. 472)
Baxter, from "Jerusalem Sonnets," 1 ("The small gray cloudy louse that nests in my beard") (p. 1267; SE p. 774)

D. The Christian Calendar

Southwell, "The Burning Babe" (p. 163; SE p. 83)
Donne, "Good Friday, 1613. Riding Westward" (p. 219; SE p. 111)
Herbert, "Easter Wings" (p. 254; SE p. 133)
Milton, "On the Morning of Christ's Nativity" (p. 279; SE p. 151)

E. The Unorthodox Clergy

Chaucer, "The Pardoner's Prologue and Tale" (p. 24; SE p. 6)
Browning, "Soliloquy of the Spanish Cloister" (p. 718; SE p. 414), "The Bishop Orders His Tomb at Saint Praxed's Church" (p. 720; SE p. 416, and "Fra Lippo Lippi" (p. 723; SE p. 419)

7.23 Youth and Age

See also Section 7.24, Children and Childhood.

Gascoigne, "Gascoigne's Lullaby" (p. 101; SE p. 57): Compare
    Hopkins's "The Habit of Perfection" (p. 854; SE p. 501),
    another series of farewells to bodily sensations.
Peele, "His Golden Locks Time Hath to Silver Turned" (p. 161; SE
    p. 82)
Shakespeare, "When That I Was and a Little Tiny Boy" (p. 195; SE
    p. 93)
Hardy, "I Look into My Glass" (p. 845; SE p. 495)
Housman, "To an Athlete Dying Young" (p. 862; SE p. 507)
Yeats, "Among School Children" (p. 888; SE p. 524) and "The Wild
    Swans at Coole" (p. 880 SE p. 516)
Frost, "Provide, Provide" (p. 921; SE p. 545): Compare Housman,
    "To an Athlete Dying Young."
Williams, "To Waken an Old Lady" (p. 944; SE p. 561)
Larkin, "Sad Steps" (p. 1231; SE p. 751)
Snodgrass, "April Inventory" (p. 1287; SE p. 783)
Hill "The Guardians" (p. 1340; SE p. 816)

A. Birthdays

Most students will have received or sent birthday greetings, and
you might ask them to bring in some greeting-card verse to
compare its methods and conventions with those of the poems
below. Most of the poems on this list mark in gloomy terms the
poet's arrival at a midpoint or crisis in his life. How is writing a
poem for your own birthday different from writing one on someone
else's?

Milton, "How Soon Hath Time" (p. 291; SE p. 163); "When I
    Consider How My Light is Spent" (p. 293; SE p. 164)
Swift, "Stella's Birthday" (p. 394; SE p. 208): Compare to Wilbur,
    "For K. R."
Byron, "On This Day I Complete My Thirty-sixth Year" (p. 612; SE
    p. 333)
Longfellow, "Mezzo Cammin" (p. 676; SE p. 382)
Housman, "Loveliest of Trees, the Cherry Now" (p. 861; SE p. 506)
Wilbur, "For K. R. on Her Sixtieth Birthday" (p. 1226; SE p. 748)

7.24 Children and Childhood

Compare poems written about children and poems written for
them (see Light Verse). See the section on Elegies for poems on
the deaths of children (3.15.B).

Blake, from *Songs of Innocence*, "Introduction" (p. 497; SE
    p. 259); "The Lamb" (p. 498; SE p. 260); "The Little Black
    Boy" (p. 499; SE p. 261): How does Blake use the black child's
    voice to suggest both his aspirations and the oppressive society
    that has shaped his vision of heaven?
Wordsworth, "It Is a Beauteous Evening" (p. 549; SE p. 284); "My
    Heart Leaps Up" (p. 551; SE p. 285); "Ode: Intimations of
    Immortality from Recollections of Early Childhood" (p. 551;
    SE p. 286)
Coleridge, "Frost at Midnight" (p. 566; SE p. 297): Compare to
    Lowell, "Harriet," for another father watching by the bed of his
    sleeping child.
Landor, "To My Child Carlino" (p. 586; SE p. 316)
Whitman, "Out of the Cradle Endlessly Rocking" (p. 770; SE
    p. 446): Compare to Wordsworth's "Ode: Intimations of
    Immortality," as accounts of childhood encounters with nature
    that shaped the adult poet.
Yeats, "The Stolen Child" (p. 875; SE p. 514); "A Prayer for My
    Daughter" (p. 884; SE p. 520)
Dunbar, "Little Brown Baby" (p. 904; SE p. 537): Compare to
    Blake's "The Little Black Boy" (p. 499; SE p. 261) Why does
    the father deliberately scare his baby with talk of the "buggah-
    man"?
Frost, "Birches" (p. 914; SE p. 541)
Ransom, "Janet Waking" (p. 1019; SE p. 617): Compare to other
    poems in which a child learns about loss, death, or separation,
    Whitman's "Out of the Cradle Endlessly Rocking," Berryman's
    "The Ball Poem," and Wilbur's "Boy at the Window."
Cummings, "in Just-" (p. 1039; SE p. 627): Compare the ways in
    which Cummings and Blake enable us to hear a child's phras-
    ings, while clearly having a control over the poem that is not
    the child's.
Roethke, "My Papa's Waltz" (p. 1117; SE p. 679)
Miles, "Find" (p. 1144; SE p. 698)
Hayden, "Those Winter Sundays" (p. 1158; SE p. 701): Compare
    the picture of love between a father and son in Roethke's "My
    Papa's Waltz."
Berryman, "The Ball Poem" (p. 1161; SE p. 704)
Thomas, "Fern Hill" (p. 1180; SE p. 716)
Lowell, "Harriet" (p. 1201; SE p. 732)
Wilbur, "Boy at the Window" (p. 1222; SE p. 746)
Kinnell, "First Song" (p. 1293; SE p. 787): Compare to E. B.
    Browning, "A Musical Instrument" (p. 675; SE p. 381), a
    mythological account of how music comes into being.
Atwood, "You Begin" (p. 1377; SE p. 838)
Ondaatje, "Burning Hills" (p. 1389; SE p. 844)

7.25 Memory

Naturally, a good number of the poems about childhood will also be poems about memory.

Vaughan, "They Are All Gone into the World of LIght!" (p. 350; SE p. 186)
Wordsworth, "Lines Composed a Few Miles Above Tintern Abbey" (p. 523; SE p. 273)
Crane, "My Grandmother's Love Letters" (p. 1054; SE p. 638)
Lowell, "My Last Afternoon with Uncle Devereux Winslow" (p. 1191; SE p. 725): Do Lowell's recollections of an uncle who died while the poet was in his early childhood include intimations of his own mortality?
Ondaatje, "Burning Hills" (p. 1389; SE p. 844)

7.26 Rich and Poor

Poetry is not written in a vacuum chamber sealed off from the facts of economic inequity. You might want to discuss with the class whether some of these poems exploit in some way the picturesque poverty of their subjects. Why do there seem to be more poems written about the poor than about the rich?

Chaucer, "Complaint to His Purse" (p. 50; SE p. 20)
Blake, "Holy Thursday [II.]" (p. 504; SE p. 262)
Wordsworth, "Resolution and Independence" (p. 546; SE p. 281): Compare to Thomas's "The Hunchback in the Park" (p. 1178; SE p. 715), with its central figure of a solitary and poor old man.
Robinson, "Richard Cory" (p. 899; SE p. 533)
Lawrence, "The English Are So Nice" (p. 955; SE p. 567): This can be a useful poem to teach in this group, as it captures the particular cadences and blindnesses of the voice of those who see themselves as privileged.
Eliot, "Sweeney Among the Nightingales" (p. 999; SE p. 598)
MacNeice, "Bagpipe Music" (p. 1113; SE p. 676)
Bishop, "Jerónimo's House" (p. 1134; SE p. 690) and "Filling Station" (p. 1139; Se p. 695)
Brooks, "kitchenette building" (p. 1182; SE p. 719) and "Boy Breaking Glass" (p. 1184; SE p. 719)

7.27 Mind and Body

In some of these poems, the mind is figured in bodily terms (Ammons), while in others the body is described in spiritual or mental terms (Donne), or is the route to an exalted state of mind (Hopkins). See also Section 7.15.D, Sex.

Donne, "The Ecstasy" (p. 213; SE p. 106): How is the speaker's characterization of the relation between mind and body designed to further his goal of seduction?

Whitman, from "Song of Myself," 24 ("Walt Whitman, a kosmos, of Manhattan the son") (p. 762; SE p. 440): Compare Whitman's devout worship of his own body ("The scent of these armpits aroma finer than prayer," line 525) to Hopkins's drive to spiritual perfection through bodily denial.

Brontë, "The Prisoner" (p. 755; SE p. 435)

Hopkins, "The Habit of Perfection" (p. 854; SE p. 501)

Ammons, "Pet Panther" (p. 1263; SE p. 771)

Bly, "Waking from Sleep" (p. 1267; SE p. 774)

Hughes, "Deaf School" (p. 1328; SE p. 808)

7.28 Sleep and Dreams

Sleep can be an escape from unpleasant waking realities (Daniel, Milton), or a visionary state akin to poetic inspiration (Coleridge, Keats). Erotic dreams lead to a rude awakening in the selections by Herrick, Milton, and Keats ("The Eve of St. Agnes").

Anonymous, "Weep You No More, Sad Fountains" (p. 88; SE p. 48)

Daniel, "Care-charmer Sleep" (p. 166; SE p. 83)

Herrick, "The Vine" (p. 242; SE p. 126)

Milton, "Methought I Saw" (p. 294; SE p. 165)

Coleridge, "Kubla Khan" (p. 564; SE p. 295)

Keats, "Ode to a Nightingale" (p. 660; SE p. 370) and "The Eve of St. Agnes" (p. 650; SE p. 360)

Jarrell, "A Girl in a Library" (p. 1166; SE p. 707)

Plath, "Sleep in the Mojave Desert" (p. 1348; SE p. 820)

7.29 Times of Day

A. Morning

Donne, "The Sun Rising" (p. 206; SE p. 101)

Herrick, "Corinna's Going A-Maying" (p. 144; SE p. 127)

Swift, "A Description of the Morning" (p. 392; SE p. 206): Compare how daybreak in Swift's city ushers in a world of false order, while in Wordsworth's it provides a fragile moment of pastoral serenity before the city wakes.

Wordsworth, "Composed upon Westminster Bridge, September 3, 1802" (p. 550; SE p. 285)

Williams, "Danse Russe" (p. 944; SE p. 560)

B. Night

What special energies does night release, or what speical knowledge does it give access to? Night may be a time of unusual serenity that yields inner peace or a sense of community, (Finch, Wordsworth, Stevens, Toomer, Gunn), or it may usher in terror or despair (Webster, Hardy).

Anonymous, "Now Go'th Sun Under Wood" (p. 3; SE p. 3)
Anonymous, "A Lyke-Wake Dirge (p. 61; SE p. 29)
Spenser, "Epithalamion" (p. 138; SE p. 68): The bridegroom's wish for night (lines 278ff.) could be taught with this group. In which poems on this list is night associated with love?
Webster, "Hark, Now Everything Is Still" (p. 241; SE p. 125)
Finch "A Nocturnal Reverie" (p. 389; SE p. 204)
Blake, "To the Evening Star" (p. 497; SE p. 259)
Shelley, "To Night" (p. 636; SE p. 353)
Wordsworth, "It Is a Beauteous Evening" (p. 549; SE p. 284)
Coleridge, "Frost at Midnight" (p. 566; SE p. 297)
Meredith, "Winter Heavens" (p. 803; SE p. 471): Compare to Frost's "Stopping By Woods," where again the serenity of evening makes a traveler question the goal of his journey.
Hardy, "In Tenebris" (p. 847; SE p. 498)
Stevens, "The House Was Quiet and the World Was Calm" (p. 936; SE p. 558)
Frost, "Stopping by Woods on a Snowy Evening" (p. 917; SE p. 542)
Toomer, "Georgia Dusk" (p. 1048; SE p. 634)
Kavanagh, "Inniskeen Road: July Evening" (p. 1087; SE p. 659)
Dickey, "In the Tree House at Night" (p. 1233; SE p. 752)
Gunn, "Back to Life" (p. 1302; SE p. 793)

7.30 The Heavens

See also Section 7.17, Science.

Sidney, *Astrophel and Stella*, 31 ("With how sad steps, O moon, thou climb'st the skies") (p. 157; SE p. 80)
Jonson, "Queen and Huntress" (p. 237; SE p. 121)
Whitman, "When I Heard the Learn'd Astronomer" (p. 764; SE p. 441)
MacNeice, "Star-gazer" (p. 1116; SE p. 678)
Larkin, "Sad Steps" (p. 1231; SE p. 751)
Rich, "Orion" (p. 1313; SE p. 797)

7.31 Chance and Destiny

This group of poems deals explicitly with large matters of the design or contingency of events and lives (issues so grand that many other poems raise them on some level). Questions of an overruling power that determines the course of events are of course a concern in many of the poems in the section on Religion (7.22).

George Meredith, "Lucifer in Starlight" (p. 803; SE p. 471)
Hardy, "Hap" (p. 844; SE p. 494) and "The Convergence of the Twain" (p. 848; SE p. 499)
Frost, "The Road Not Taken" (p. 913; SE p. 540) and "Design" (p. 921; SE p. 545): In what sense is "Design" a miniaturized version of Hardy's "The Convergence of the Twain"?
William Meredith, "Accidents of Birth" (p. 1211; SE p. 739)

7.32 Solitude

These poems present solitude in a number of ways: as utter isolation from all other beings (Cowper, Arnold, Clare, Dickinson), or as pensive serenity (Milton, Yeats, Bly), or as a perilously tempting wavering between the two (Frost, "Stopping by Woods").

Milton, "Il Penseroso" (p. 287; SE p. 159)
Cowper, "The Castaway" (p. 485; SE p. 257)
Wordsworth, "I Wandered Lonely as a Cloud (p. 556; SE p. 290)
Clare, "I Am" (p. 646; SE p. 358)
Arnold, "To Marguerite" (p. 783; SE p. 457)
Dickinson, Poem 303 ("The Soul selects her own Society—") (p. 807; SE p. 475)
Yeats, "The Lake Isle of Innisfree" (p. 876; SE p. 515)
Frost, "Stopping By Woods on a Snowy Evening" (p. 917; SE p. 532) and "The Most of It" (p. 923; SE p. 546)
Hugo, "Salt Water Story" (p. 1244; SE p. 759)
Bly, "Driving Toward the Lac Qui Parle River" (p. 1268; SE p. 775)
O'Hara, "How to Get There" (p. 1286; SE p. 782)

7.33 Death

This list is limited to poems that reflect on death in a general way, rather than mourn a particular death; for the latter see Elegies (3.15). Poems on mortality, mutability, and transience are included. You might compare poems that welcome death or that arrive at some sort of acceptance of it (Nashe, Bradstreet, Landor, Keats) and those that resist or defy it (Donne, Thomas, Berryman).

Nashe, "A Litany in Time of Plague" (p. 202; SE p. 98)
Donne, "Holy Sonnets," 10 ("Death be not proud, though some
    have called thee" (p. 222; SE p. 113)
Bradstreet, "The Vanity of All Worldly Things" (p. 322; SE p. 168)
Johnson, "The Vanity of Human Wishes" (p. 451; SE p. 238)
Landor, "Dying Speech of an Old Philosopher" (p. 587; SE p. 318)
Keats, "When I Have Fears" (p. 649; SE p. 359)
Lawrence, "The Ship of Death" (p. 957; SE p. 569)
Housman, "From Far, from Eve and Morning" (p. 864; SE p. 509):
    Compare Meredith, "Accidents of Birth" (p. 1211; SE p. 739)
Berryman, from "The Dream Songs," 382 ("At Henry's bier let
    some thing fall out well") (p. 1165; SE p. 706)
Thomas, "Do Not Go Gentle into That Good Night" (p. 1181; SE
    p. 718)
Plath, "Lady Lazarus" (p. 1354; SE p. 824)

7.34 A World Beyond

Not poems about an afterlife or resurrection, these poems envision
a realm where questions of life and death, faith and doubt, society
and solitude, etc., seem to lose their urgency: utopian imaginings.

Herrick, "The White Island, or Place of the Blest" (p. 250; SE
    p. 132)
Marvell, "Bermudas" (p. 336; SE p. 177) and "The Garden"
    (p. 343; SE p. 182)
Coleridge, "Kubla Khan" (p. 564; SE p. 295)
Blake, from Milton, "And Did Those Feet" (p. 510; SE p. 266)
Yeats, "The Lake Isle of Innisfree" (p. 876; SE p. 515), "Sailing to
    Byzantium" (p. 886; SE p. 522), and "Byzantium" (p. 890; SE
    p. 525)
Walcott, "The Season of Phantasmal Peace" (p. 1339; SE p. 815)

8 TRADITION, INNOVATIONS, AND REVISIONS

8.1 Allusion

Dickinson, Poem 1545 ("The Bible is an antique volume") (p. 816;
SE p. 478) and Watts, "Our God, Our Help" (p. 400; SE p. 209): On
some level all of Dickinson's poems may be considered allusion
to— and revisions if not parodies of— the neat, faithful hymns of
Watts, among others. Rejecting the unquestioning pieties of Watts,
Dickinson twists his meter, which had been regular to make it
singable by a congregation. What changes would have to be made to
the Watts poem to make it into a Dickinson poem?

Housman, "Is My Team Plowing" (p. 863; SE p. 508) and Popular
Ballads (pp. 68-84; SE pp. 34-46): Which ballads is Housman's
updated version responding to most closely? Compare
Housman's updating of the ballad and Auden's in "As I Walked
Out One Evening" (p. 1099; SE p. 667).
Pound, "Envoi" from "Hugh Selwyn Mauberley" (p. 971; SE p. 583)
and Waller, "Song" ("Go, lovely rose!") (p. 274; SE p. 146)
Eliot, "The Waste Land" (p. 1000; SE p. 599): A pervasively and
deeply allusive poem; what sorts of demands does such erudite
poetry place upon the reader? Which of Eliot's own footnotes
to the poem are seriously useful references, and which are
jokes upon learned annotations?
MacLeish, "You, Andrew Marvell" (p. 1030; SE p. 621) and Marvell,
"To His Coy Mistress" (p. 337; SE p. 178)
Auden, "As I Walked Out One Evening" (p. 1099; SE p. 667) and
Popular Ballads (pp. 68-84; SE pp. 34-46).
Lowell, "The Quaker Graveyard in Nantucket" (p. 1185; SE p. 720)
and Longfellow, "The Jewish Cemetery at Newport" (p. 677;
SE p. 382)
Levertow, "O Taste and See" (p. 1248; SE p. 761) and Wordsworth,
"The World Is Too Much with Us" (p. 559; SE p. 292)
Heaney, from *Glanmore Sonnets*, 10 ("I dreamt we slept in a moss
in Donegal") (p. 1386: SE p. 843) and Wyatt, "They Flee From
Me" (p. 91; SE p. 50): What is the function of Heaney's allusion
("how like you this?") to Wyatt's sonnet? Does this linkage of a
phrase suggest deeper affinities between these two poems?

A. Epigraphs

A number of nineteenth-century poems and a larger number of
twentiety-century poems that do not explicitly cite a source within
the poem itself may allude to some earlier text through the use of
an epigraph or motto— a brief quotation placed at the head of the

poem. What diverse relations may obtain between poem and epigraph? Does the poem illustrate the epigraph, contemplate it, revise it, or simply use it as an inviting or intriguing introduction into the poem? When may the epigraph function as an alternative title? See also the section on Beginnings (4.2).

Wordsworth, "Ode: Intimations of Immortality" (p. 551; SE p. 286): Why is it appropriate for this poem to have as an epigraph a passage from an earlier poem by Wordsworth himself?

Coleridge, "The Rime of the Ancient Mariner" (p. 567; SE p. 298). The epigraph to "Dejection: An Ode" (p. 581; SE p. 312) is from the popular ballad "Sir Patrick Spens" (p. 74; SE p. 38), in a version somewhat different from the one in the anthology.

Landor, "To My Child Carlino" (p. 586; SE p. 316)

Shelley, "Adonais" (p. 626; SE p. 343)

Tennyson, "Mariana" (p. 698; SE p. 396)

Hardy, "In Tenebris" (p. 847; SE p. 498): Compare to other poems headed by epigraphs from scripture, such as Hopkin's "[Thou Art Indeed Just, Lord ...]" (p. 860; SE p. 506), Everson's "In All These Acts" (p. 1147; SE p. 700), Lowell's "The Quaker Graveyard in Nantucket" (p. 1185; SE p. 720), and Hollander's "Adam's Task" (p. 1306; SE p. 795)

Pound, "The Garden" (p. 962; SE p. 575), "Hugh Selwyn Mauberley" (p. 964; SE p. 576)

Eliot, "The Love Song of J. Alfred Prufrock" (p. 994; SE p. 594); "Sweeney Among the Nightingales" (p. 999; SE p. 598); "The Waste Land" (p. 1000; SE p. 599)

MacDiarmid, "In the Children's Hospital" (p. 1027; SE p. 620)

Warren, "Sila" (p. 1091; SE p. 662)

Reed, from Lessons of the War (p. 1171; SE p. 730): What is the effect of the change Reed makes in the lines from Horace?

Lowell, "For the Union Dead" (p. 1198; SE p. 730): What is the effect of heading a poem with an inscription from a monument?

Meredith, "Accidents of Birth" (p. 1211; SE p. 739): Do the two weighty epigraphs make the poem top-heavy? How might we read the poem differently without the epigraphs, or with only one of them?

Wilbur, "Junk" (p. 1224; SE p. 747)

Hill, From "An Apology for the Revival of Christian Architecture in England" (p. 1344; SE p. 818)

Stallworthy, "The Source" (p. 1365; SE p. 831): How does the epigraph add the solidity and authority of Yeats's voice to the poem's outcries of instinct?

Heaney, "The Strand at Lough Beg" (p. 1384; SE p. 841)

Voight, "Rescue" (p. 1394; SE p. 847)

8.2 Parody

Herrick, "Delight in Disorder" (p. 243; SE p. 126) and Jonson, "Still
   To Be Neat" (p. 238; SE p. 122)
Carroll, "The White Knight's Song" (p. 827; SE p. 483) and Words-
   worth, "Resolution and Independence" (p. 546; SE p. 281)
Lewis, "Song" ("Come live with me and be my love") (p. 1081; SE
   p. 657); Marlowe, "The Passionate Shepherd to His Love"
   (p. 185; SE p. 87); and Ralegh, "The Nymph's Reply to the
   Shepherd" (p. 105; SE p. 58)
Koch, "Variations on a Theme by William Carlos Williams" (p. 1253;
   SE p. 763) and Williams, "This Is Just to Say" (p. 945; SE
   p. 562)

8.3 Mythology

A. Classical Mythology

This group includes poems that mourn the passing of "a creed outworn" (Wordsworth, Poe), or others that find in the Greek deities a
"mighty lesson" (Byron). Others debunk the old myths as "an over-
heated farmhand's literature" (Walcott) or as a perpetuation of
outmoded or oppressive ways of thinking (Rich).

Milton, "Oh the Morning of Christ's Nativity" (p. 279; SE p. 151):
   The birth of the Christ child routs all the pagan deities,
   scattering them from the woods and altars they inhabited. The
   nymphs and dryads of classical mythology are banished, it
   seems, to poetry itself; thus Milton can compare the infant
   Christ with the infant Hercules, who strangled a snake in his
   cradle (lines 226-228). Compare to Poe, "Sonnet—To Science"
   where again the dryad is banished from the wood, but by a
   different force.
Wordsworth, "The World Is Too Much With Us" (p. 559; SE
   p. 292): Compare the solace Wordsworth seeks in a "creed
   outworn" to other uses the poets on this list find for classical
   myths. Ask students to reflect on the difference between such
   capitalized powers as "Nature" and the "Sea" to "Proteus" and
   "Triton." Compare with Walcott, "Europa" as meditations on
   mythology that begin in a landscape in which the appeal of the
   old myths becomes apparent.
Byron, "Prometheus" (p. 591; SE p. 320): Compare Byron's suffering
   immortal with Tennyson's Tithonus, who has also been granted
   what Byron calls "the wretched gift eternity" (line 24).
Keats, "To Homer" (p. 649; SE p. 360) and "On First Looking into
   Chapman's Homer" (p. 648; SE p. 359): Keats links blind
   Homer's vision with a special access to the Greek deities.
   Compare what Keats reads Homer for, as suggested in these
   sonnets, with what Tennyson and Pound read him for, as

suggested in their poems based on Homeric epic in the next section.

Poe, "Sonnet—To Science" (p. 694; SE p. 393): If Poe berates science for destroying mythology, why does he still use mythological figures such as "Old Time"? "Science" herself becomes a mythological figure with an appropriate ancestry: you might ask students who Science's other parent might be, on the model of Keats's Grecian Urn as foster-child of silence and slow time. What is the function of the hint of the myth of Prometheus in lines 3-4? You might refer to Byron's "Prometheus" in posing this question.

Poe, "Helen" (p. 979; SE p. 394): A woman who is like the women of classical myth is also like a work of art, a posed statue. In the stasis and balance of the last stanza in particular, the poem my be compared with Bogan, "Medusa" and Yeats, "Leda and the Swan."

Tennyson, "Tithonus" (p. 713; SE p. 411): In his longing for the kind respite of mortality, and his temptations from an immortal lover, Tithonus may be compared to the Odysseus of MacLeish and Merwin in the next group.

Yeats, "Leda and the Swan" (p. 888; SE p. 523)

Robinson, "Miniver Cheevy" (p. 900; SE p. 533): What values did Miniver hold when he "dreamed of Thebes and Camelot / And Priam's neighbors"?

Bogan, "Medusa" (p. 1052; SE p. 637): Does Medusa's gaze turn the world into timeless art or sterile, deathly stasis? Compare the unmoving scene in the poem with the narrative liveliness of the painting in Auden, "Musée."

Auden, "Musée des Beaux Arts" (p. 1100; SE p. 668)

Rich, "Orion" (p. 1313, SE p. 797): Like Walcott in "Europa," Rich reflects on a myth by looking at a constellation. What outworn creeds does Orion perpetuate?

Walcott, "Europa" (p. 1338; SE p. 814): Compare with Poe, "Sonnet— to Science" as a debunking of mythology that is still enamored of it. Compare Walcott's treatment of the myth of the coupling of a woman and a god in beast's disguise with Yeats, "Leda and the Swan."

Simic, "Charon's Cosmology" (p. 1372; SE p. 835)

B. The Myth of Odysseus

Poems about Odysseus may stress his striving imagination (Daniel, Tennyson) or his human, homing temperament (MacLeish, Merwin). Compare the poems that imagine Odysseus' setting forth (Tennyson, Pound) and those that focus on his return (MacLeish, Merwin). Poems about how the hero resists the seductions of repose during his long homecoming (Daniel, MacLeish) might be compared with other poems about the temptations of respite from other kinds of journeys, such as Frost's "Stopping by Woods on a Snowy Evening."

Daniel, "Ulysses and the Siren" (p. 166; SE p. 84): Daniel borrows
figures from Homeric epic to stage a debate between the principles of ease and action. Daniel's Ulysses advocates unrest
and toil in terms so like those of Tennyson's Ulysses that
passages from these two poems might be paired as a study in
how different meters accomodate similar ideas.
Tennyson, "Ulysses" (p. 704; SE p. 402) and "The Lotos-Eaters"
(p. 700; SE p. 398)
Pound, Canto I ("And then went down to the ship") (p. 976; SE
p. 583)
MacLeish, "Calypso's Island" (p. 1031; SE p. 622)
Merwin, "Odysseus" (p. 1296; SE p. 789)

C. Other Mythologies

Yeats, "The Stolen Child" (p. 875; SE p. 514), "The Circus
Animals' Desertion" (p. 894; SE p. 529)
Hill, from *Mercian Hymns* (p. 1341; SE p. 816)
Klein, "Indian Reservation: Caughnawaga" (p. 1124; SE 684)

8.4 Biblical Stories

This topic about the traditions upon which poems may draw is, of
course, very close to the topic of Religion (Section 7.22). But I
think it is worth isolating— particularly in the context of studying
the uses of classical mythology in poetry— uses of scriptural
mythological, or biblical narratives. How do poets treat classical
tales differently from biblical tales? Why is the Book of Genesis
such a fruitful source for poetry?

Anonymous, "Adam Lay I-bounden" (p. 53; SE p. 23)
Dickinson, Poem 1545 ("The Bible is an antique Volume") (p. 816;
SE p. 478)
Yeats, "The Second Coming" (p. 883; SE p. 520)
Muir, "The Animals" (p. 991; SE p. 592)
Hope, "Imperial Adam" (p. 1111; SE p. 674)
Nemerov, "The Historical Judas" (p. 1218; SE p. 743)
Hollander, "Adam's Task" (p. 1306; SE p. 795)

8.5 Occasion

Although this is a large topic, it is one that can be useful at the
beginning of a poetry survey. Students coming to their first college
course on poetry may be asking, Why do poets write poems at all?
Does a poet need a reason to write a poem? What sorts of things
happening in the world at large can be a sufficient goad to get a

poem started? Rather than treat what is conventionally termed "occasional poetry" (verse commissioned for, or written to commemorate, a public event such as a coronation, holiday, anniversary) as a separate mode, I prefer to introduce it as a specific answer to a large question about the range of stimuli that may spark a poem into being written. It is important for beginning students to learn that poems can be occasioned by events as dissimilar in nature and scope as the sight of a rainbow and the advent of a season, the death of a pet rabbit and the massacre of huge numbers of people. (Elegies could be fruitfully included in this topic.) The urge to write a poem is as varied as the impetus behind any kind of utterance: to celebrate something, to console oneself, to pray, to commemorate, to praise. Or a poet may write to correct what a poet may see as errors in earlier poems, or to register pleasure in the act of poetry-making itself.

It is not always easy to distinguish between a poem's occasion and what we more simply call its subject or topic of concern, but here I have isolated poems that announce themselves as responses to some quite specific *occasion*, including the special sense of holiday or marked day on the calendar. Nor is it always easy to distinguish between a poem's real occasion and the fictions of its occasion it may suggest.

A. Private Occasions (See also Birthdays, Section 7.23. A)

Bradstreet, "Here Follow's Some Verses Upon the Burning of Our House, July 10th, 1666" (p. 325; SE p. 170)
Wordsworth, "Composed upon Westminster Bridge, September 3, 1802" (p. 550; SE p. 285)
Williams, "This Is Just to Say" (p. 945; SE p. 562)

B. Public Occasions: War and Politics (See also Section 7.5, War, and Section 7.17, Social and Political Protest.)

Milton, "On the Late Massacre in Piedmont" (p. 293; SE p. 164)
Collins, "Ode Written in the Beginning of the Year 1746" (p. 467; SE p. 251)
Emerson, "Concord Hymn: Sung at the Completion of the Battle Monument, July 4, 1837" (p. 665; SE p. 375): Why does Emerson mention that the famous bridge on this site is no longer there? In what sense will the newly completed monument replace the ruined bridge? This poem has been inscribed on the Concord Monument.

An exercise: in conjunction with the poems in this group, and Emerson's in particular, it can be helpful to assign students to look for and copy down commemorative inscriptions on university buildings or monuments (buildings or other structures that were class-gifts often bear verses or other inscriptions). Compare how these local inscriptions take up the task of marking a commemorative occasion and marking the building or structure as a site for commemoration.

Hardy, "The Convergence of the Twain: Lines on the Loss of the Titantic" (p. 848; SE p. 499): To illustrate the wide range of possible poetic occasions, compare Hardy's poem on a monumental, tragic, and public convergence with Frost's miniture drama of convergence, "Design" (p. 921; SE p. 545).
Yeats, "Easter 1916" (p. 881; SE p. 518)

8.6 Translations

Can a poem that is translated from another languate into English be an English poem in its own right? Even if you cannot teach the original poem, you can use these poems to introduce different approaches to translation, perhaps also by bringing to the students' attention other translations of these poems for comparison. Questions of translation are useful for teaching lyric poetry in general: ask students which part of a poem they think would be the hardest to translate into another language, or which poets they think would be hardest to translate. Why might Cummings or Dickinson be harder to translate than Stevens? What different features of the poetry would be likely to be lost in translating a poem by Wyatt and a poem by Blake? What different features would be lost when an English poem is translated into French, Spanish, or German? Even if students have just a year or so of a foreign language, they may find it instructive to cast a stanza or two of an English poem into that language, or from that language into English (perhaps working collaboratively), and discuss the results. In conjunction with this topic, see Keats's "On First Looking into Chapman's Homer" (p. 648; SE p. 359), about the experience of reading a formerly inaccessible poet through a good translation.

Poems in the anthology that are translations— of varying degrees of accuracy and freedom— are listed here. Some may be more aptly called adaptations, variations, or imitations than translations. Elizabeth Barrett Browning's "Sonnets from the Portuguese" (p. 674; SE p. 380) are not actually translations of Portuguese texts: why might a poet title her work as though they were English versions of works in another language?

Wyatt, "The Long Love That in My Thought Doth Harbor" (p. 89; SE p. 49): From the Italian of Petrarch. Compare Surrey's translation of the same sonnet.
Surrey, "Love, That Doth Reign and Live Within My Thought" (p. 98; SE p. 54)
Campion, "My Sweetest Lesbia" (p. 198; SE p. 95)

Jonson, "Come, My Celia" (p. 237 SE p. 121): Lines 6-8 are recognizably versions of the same moment in Catullus that Campion draws upon in lines 3-7 of "My Sweetest Lesbia" (p. 198; SE p. 95).

Fitzgerald, "The Rubáiyát of Omar Khayyán of Naishápúr" (p. 684; SE p. 384)

Yeats, "When You Are Old and Gray and Full of Sleep" (p. 876; SE p. 514): From the French of Ronsard

Pound, "The Seafarer" (p. 1031; SE p. 572)

Wilbur, "Junk" (p. 1224; SE p. 747): Compare to Pound's version of Old English alliterative verse in "The Seafarer."

9 MINORITY VOICES

9.1 Women Poets

A number of women poets in the anthology's selections write about the condition of being female (Elizabeth I, Montagu, Millay, Rich, Page, Lorde, Atwood). Are there other subjects common to women's poetry? One must hesitate to generalize on the basis of these selections, of course, but you might speculate on why there are several poems about animals in this group, including Dickinsons's "A Bird Came Down the Walk" (p. 808; SE p. 475) and "A narrow Fellow in the Grass" (p. 814; SE p. 477), Moore's "Peter" (p. 989; SE p. 591), Bishop's "The Fish" (p. 1136; SE p. 692), Plath's "Black Rook in Rainy Weather" (p. 1345; SE p. 818), and Atwood's "The Animals in that Country" (p. 1374; SE p. 836) and "Pig Song" (p. 1376; SE p. 837). Are animals a favored subject for women poets because they provide useful masks or mouthpieces for women's own voices? Or is it rather that women's poems about animals are the ones that tend to be anthologized (assuming anthologizers to be male and compiling their selections for a male audience?), because they seem less threatening and direct than other of their poems, more distanced from the issues of women poets as such and hence from a range of potentially explosive topics?

Larger questions include whether there are special measures whereby women's voices, traditionally silenced, can gain poetic authority. What sorts of speakers are featured in these poems? Plath gives a voice to a tree ("Elm," p. 1351; SE p. 821), Atwood to a pig ("Pig Song," p. 1376; SE p. 837); this group also includes poems that are fictively uttered by a poolroom gang (Brooks's "We Real Cool," p. 1183; SE p. 719), by a dead person (Dickinson's "I heard a Fly buzz— when I died—" and "Because I could not stop for Death—"; Atwood's "This Is a Photograph of Me"), by a prisoner (Brontë's "The Prisoner"). How might such fictive speakers enable a woman poet to speak more freely and boldly than if she speaks in a less mediated verson of her own voice? Must or do we always think of the "I" who speaks in women's poems as a female "I"? (More so than we think of the "I" in men's poems as male?) What strategic use of poetic forms might women poets make in order to free and amplify their voices? A wide range of intricate forms are represented, including Dickinson's unorthodox private hymns, Marianne Moore's syllabic verses, the sonnets of E. B. Browning, Rosetti, Millay, Bishop's "Sestina" (p. 1142; SE p. 697), and Bogan's "Song for the Last Act" (p. 1053; SE p. 638).

An exercise for airing assumptions and prejudices is to give students copies of poems whose author is not indicated, but tell them that some of the poems were written by men and some by women and ask them to identify which is which, and give their reasons. Or you can be even trickier: distribute in class unidentified copies of some of the poems from this list, and some unlabeled poems by men, but tell them that the women's poems are written by men and vice versa, and ask students what clues they can find that might have let them identify the authors by sex. I suspect that most classes will have no difficulty finding signs of "feminine" style in some of the men's poems, and a "masculine" manner in the women's poems, if you hint that they will find them. Such an exercise might then enable the class to investigate with a fresher eye questions such as whether there are stylistic affinities among these women poets, whether "writing like a woman" is a phrase that means anything.

In the list below I have suggested groupings and comparisons among the selections by women poets.

Elizabeth I (p. 100; SE p. 55)

Anne Bradstreet (p. 322; SE p. 168): You might want to begin a unit on women poets with selections on poetry or artistic creation, such as Bradstreet's "The Author to Her Book" (p. 324; SE p. 169), Dickinson's "Tell all the Truth but tell it slant—" (p. 815; SE p. 478), H. D.'s "Wine Bowl" (p. 980; SE p. 586), Moore's "Poetry" (p. 986; SE p. 590), Rich's "Aunt Jennifer's Tigers" (p. 1309; SE p. 796), and Silko's "How to Write a Poem about the Sky" (p.1401; SE p. 852).

Ann Finch, Countess of Winchilsea (p. 389; SE p. 204)

Lady Mary Wortley Montagu (p. 441; SE p. 237): "The Lover: A Ballad" could be taught in the context of other poems in which women define what they do and do not want from men, including Millay's "I, Being Born a Woman and Distressed" (p. 1033; SE p. 624), Parker's "One Perfect Rose" (p. 1038; SE p. 627), Rich's "Living in Sin" (p. 1309; SE p. 797).

Elizabeth Barrett Browning (p. 674; SE p. 380)

Emily Brontë (p. 753; SE p. 435): You might ask the class to speculate about why "No Coward Soul Is Mine" (p. 756; SE p. 436) was one of Dickinson's favorite poems.

Emily Dickinson (p. 804; SE p. 472)

Christina Rossetti (p. 817; SE p. 479): Compare "Song" ("When I am dead, my dearest") to Dickinson's poems spoken from the grave ("I heard a Fly buzz—when I died—" (p. 809; SE p. 476) and "Because I could not stop for Death—" (p. 812; SE p. 476) and to Plath's "Lady Lazarus" (p. 1354; SE p. 824).

H. D. (p. 978; SE p. 585): Compare "Wine Bowl" to other poems about art and artifacts, such as Moore's "No Swan so Fine" (p. 987; SE p. 591) and Rich's "Aunt Jennifer's Tigers" (p. 1309; SE p. 796), perhaps with a glance at Keats's "Ode on a Grecian Urn" (p. 663; SE p. 372).

Marianne Moore (p. 986; SE p. 590)

Edna St. Vincent Millay (p. 1032; SE p. 623): Compare the image of
the sea and the world under the sea in "Above These Cares" (p.
1034; SE p. 624) to Bishop's "At the Fishhouse" (p. 1138; SE
p. 693), Rich's "Diving into the Wreck" (p. 1315; SE
p. 798), Atwood's "This Is a Photograph of Me" (p. 1373; SE
p. 836), and Silko's "Prayer to the Pacific" (p. 1402; SE
p. 853).
Dorothy Parker (p. 1038; SE p. 626)
Louise Bogan (p. 1052; SE p. 637)
Stevie Smith (p. 1072; SE p. 651): Compare the critique of
conventional religion in "No Categories!" (p. 1072; SE p. 651)
to Dickinson's "The Bible is an antique Volume—" (p. 816; SE
p. 478)
Elizabeth Bishop (p. 1133; SE p. 690)
Josephine Miles (p. 1143; SE p. 698): Compare "Memorial Day" to
Levertov's "Tenebrae" (p. 1249; SE p. 762)
Gwendolyn Brooks (p. 1182; SE p. 719): Compare the picture of
domestic poverty in "kitchenette building" (p. 1182; SE
p. 719) with the cozy clutter of Bishop's "Jerónimo's House"
(p. 1134; SE p. 690).
P. K. Page (p. 1203; SE p. 735)
Denise Levertov (p. 1245; SE p. 760)
Adrienne Rich (p. 1309; SE p. 796)
Sylvia Plath (p. 1345; SE p. 813): Compare Plath's bitter poems
about powerful male archetypes such as "The Colossus" and
"Daddy," to Rich's "Orion" (p. 1313; SE p. 797).
Audre Lorde (p. 1362; SE p. 829)
Margaret Atwood (p. 1373; SE p. 836)
Ellen Bryant Voigt (p. 1393; SE p. 847): Compare "Rescue" to
Atwood's "You Begin" (p. 1377; SE p. 838) and Silko's "How
to Write a Poem about the Sky" (p. 1401; SE p. 852); compare
the tone with which the "you" (presumably a child or
children) is addressed in each.
Leslie Marmon Silko (p. 1401; SE p. 852)

A. Poems about Women

Women poets are not the only ones who write about the plight of
women. I have grouped here a number of poems by men that
acknowledge some of the same contradictions and hardships of
women's lives that concern women poets, such as the harsh stan-
dards by which women's sexual behavior is judged (Goldsmith,
Hardy, Heaney) and the burdens their own sexuality can put upon
them in a man's world (Berryman). You might discuss in class
whether the poems that stress the narrowness or shallowness of
women's lives (Cummings, Jarrell) should be considered to
condemn women or to expose and thereby condemn the social
conditions that so constrict their lives.

A number of love poems could also be useful in teaching this group (see Section 7.15). For other poems about women, see also sections on the Muse (7.2), Home and Family Life (7.7), Women and Art (7.18.A), and Song (3.8), which includes a number of poems about women singing.

Anonymous, "Mary Hamilton" (p. 80; SE p. 42)
Suckling, "Upon My Lady Carlisle's Walking in Hampton Court Garden" (p. 318; SE p. 166): This can be a revealing poem to teach with this group, as it provides the rare opportunity of eavesdropping on two men discussing a woman's body.
Marvell, "The Gallery" (p. 338; SE p. 179)
Pope, "Epistle to Miss Blount" (p. 423; SE p. 226)
Goldsmith, "When Lovely Woman Stoops to Folly" (p. 472; SE p. 255)
Blake, "A Question Answered" (p. 508; SE p. 266)
Hardy, "The Ruined Maid" (p. 847; SE p. 497)
Yeats, "Adam's Curse" (p. 879; SE p. 516) and "A Prayer for My Daughter" (p. 884: SE p. 520)
Williams, "The Young Housewife" (p. 944; SE p. 560)
Cummings, "the Cambridge ladies who live in furnished souls" (p. 1041; SE p. 628)
Berryman, from "The Dream Songs," 375 ("His Helplessness") (p. 1165; SE p. 706)
Jarrell, "A Girl in a Library" (p. 1166; SE p. 707)
Heaney, "Punishment" (p. 1382; SE p. 839)

9.2 Black Poets

The state of being black is an explicit subject of many of these poems. As for women poets, larger questions include the strategies whereby black poets, marginalized in white culture, can gain power and authority for their utterances and visions. In what ways do all these poets confront the question Hughes asks in "Theme for English B" (p. 1069; SE p. 648), "will my page be colored that I write?" The forms chosen by black poets range from the balanced pentameter quatrains of Toomer's "Georgia Duck" (p. 1048; SE p. 634), the throbbing trochaic couplets of Cullen's "Heritage" (p. 1076; SE p. 653), the Whitmanian catalogues of Hughes's "The Negro Speaks of Rivers" (p. 1067; SE p. 648), to what Hayden calls the "sad blackface lilt and croon" ("Paul Lawrence Dunbar," p. 1161; SE p. 703) of Dunbar's poems in black dialect; other black poets play with a mixture of standard, even elevated language and direct, informal slang, as in Reed's "beware : do not read this poem."
    In the list below I have suggested comparisons between the selections by black poets.

Paul Lawrence Dunbar (p. 904; SE p. 537): In what sense is Dunbar's use of black English in "Little Brown Baby" an act of wearing "a mask that grins and lies" ("We Wear the Mask")? In what sense is it an act of pulling off a mask?

Jean Toomer (p. 1047; SE p. 634): Compare the mixture of the mill workers' "race memories" and "dreams of Christ" in "Georgia Dusk" to Cullen's concern in "Heritage" (p. 1076; SE p. 653) with his divided allegiance to an African past and a Christian faith.

Langston Hughes (p. 1067; SE p. 647): Compare "The Weary Blues" to other poems in which black voices are most powerfully heard in song, such as Toomer's "Georgia Dusk" (p. 1048; SE p. 634).

Countee Cullen (p. 1076; SE p. 653)

Robert Hayden (p. 1158; SE p. 701): Hayden's tribute to Dunbar raises questions of the literary models and influences, white and black, available to and adopted by black poets. As a black poet, what does Hayden admire about Dunbar?

Gwendolyn Brooks (p. 1182: SE p. 719): Compare the broken window as a "cry of art" in "Boy Breaking Glass" to Baraka's suggestion that the (black?) poet's art is the ability to say "Let's Pretend" in "In Memory of Radio" (p. 1356; SE p. 826).

Derek Walcott (p. 1333; SE p. 812)

Amiri Baraka (p. 1356: SE p. 826): Compare the charged sense of the word "dream" in "The New World" with the resonance that word has in Hughes's "Harlem" (p. 1069; SE p. 648) and Brooks's "kitchenette building" (p. 1182; SE p. 719).

Audre Lorde (p. 1362; SE p. 829)

Ishmael Reed (p. 1368: SE p. 834): Compare the claims Reed makes for the bodily presence of the reader in "beware : do not read this poem" with the sexual writing ("my body / writes into your flesh") of Lorde's "Recreation" (p. 1363; SE p. 830); compare both to Ashbery's "Paradoxes and Oxymorons" (p. 1292; SE p. 787) and Stevens's "The House was Quiet and the World Was Calm" (p. 936; SE p. 558). Why does Reed see the oneness of his poem and his reader as dangerous, while Ashbery and Stevens do not?

A. Poems about Race and Racism

Blake, "The Little Black Boy" (p. 499; SE p. 261)

Kipling, "Recessional" (p. 870; SE p. 513): This celebration of British imperial power, won by dominating those whom the conquerors could conveniently label "lesser breeds without the Law," can be an instructive poem to teach in the context of questions of race. For the self-serving voice of imperialism, or

at least of racial chauvinism, laid bare, compare Lawrence's "The English Are So Nice!" (p. 955; SE p. 567).
Klein, "Indian Reservation: Caughnawaga" (p. 1124; SE p. 684)

9.3 Canadian Poets

E. J. Pratt (p. 938; SE p. 559)
Earle Birney (p. 1079; SE p. 656)
A. M. Klein (p. 1124; SE p. 684)
P. K. Page (1203; SE p. 735)
Al Purdy (p. 1205; SE p. 736)
Leonard Cohen (p. 1360; SE p. 828)
Margaret Atwood (p. 1373; SE p. 836)
Michael Ondaatje (p. 1387; SE p. 844)
Tom Wayman (p. 1398; SE p. 850)

INDEX OF AUTHORS AND POEMS DISCUSSED